DEAD LIONS

By

A.D. Winans

Punk ♣ Hostage ♣ Press

Dead Lions

ISBN-10: 1940213940
ISBN-13: 978-1-940213-94-1

First Edition

Cover Design by A. Razor
Introduction by John Dorsey

Photo of Bob Kaufman by A.D.Winans
Photo of Jack Micheline by A.D.Winans
Photo of A.D. Winans and Jack Micheline by Linda
Learner

Punk Hostage Press
P.O. Box 1869
Hollywood CA 90078
www.punkhostagepress.com

The American Poetry Review, The Chiron Review, and Dust-
Books published some of the work in this book. Grateful
acknowledgement is made to the publishers and editors.

Introduction

Dead Lions still roar: On the writing of A.D. Winans

A.D. Winans knows a little something about literary lions and the sounds their pens make. For those of you who're only familiar with Winans' poetry or his work with the now legendary Second Coming Press, this book offers something truly special, a glimpse into the lives and careers of four very different writers, whose friendship, encouragement, and personal courage, not only helped shape him as an artist, but also as a human being and concerned citizen of the world.

I don't think it's a coincidence that Winans begins his book talking about Academy Award nominated screenwriter and novelist Alvah Bessie. From the very beginning he talks about how many younger people may not even be familiar with the sinister patriotism known as the House Un-American Activities Committee (HUAC) and the sacrifices made for our personal freedoms by a group of writers known as "The Hollywood Ten." I'd like to tell him he's wrong, but if I'm being honest, the acts of these brave men now seem largely forgotten by those of my own generation, relegated to the dusty e-books of history. Bessie in particular gets cast aside for splashier figures such as Dalton Trumbo or Ring Lardner, Jr., but as Winans shows us, all of these men were freedom fighters that paid dearly for their principles and while writers in other genres such as literary fiction or poetry can experience a sort of renaissance of public awareness, this is rarely the case of the Hollywood screenwriter, who today more than ever--is usually the forgotten man or woman on any studio lot. So Winans has decided to throw Bessie's hat back into the ring, to bring his name and life's work back into the conversation, to keep his memory alive by infusing his own personal story and experiences with the man and I'm glad he has.

He continues the book talking about the late street poet Jack Micheline. Born in 1929, Micheline was anti-establishment even in the world of the anti-establishment, rejecting the label of "beat" and the cottage of industry of cool that came with it during the 1950's and 1960's.

Roaming the Earth in the tradition of Walt Whitman and early 20th century troubadour Vachel Lindsay, Micheline liked to spread his work around publishing in small presses and printing his own books to sell in exchange for food and a place to sleep.

Unlike Bessie, Micheline's work has never had a very large stage, but what unites these two great men is not their place in history or even their place in Mr. Winans' creative life, but their willingness to go against the grain and risk the creature comforts that many of us take for granted.

The same could be said of the poet Bob Kaufman, whose life fills the pages in the third section of this book. A political and spiritual revolutionary of words, Kaufman could and perhaps should be seen as the Godfather of the modern spoken word movement and Winans tells his story as only a true friend could tell it, with love, honesty, and respect for a man who published little in his own lifetime.

The last author discussed in this book is forgotten by no one, particularly the young, and as such his inclusion here may seem out of place to some readers. I'm talking, of course, about Charles Bukowski. Everybody knows Bukowski, the poet, novelist and screenwriter who needs no renaissance, because his reputation grows deservedly stronger every day. The problem is, that's all many readers see, the fame, the money that came later in life and the romanticism in tiny rooms soaked in booze and madness. Unlike the other writers in this book Bukowski doesn't need people to remember his work, but remember that he was a human being, that he wrote poems, that he wrote fiction, but that the madness was in large part, real and that there was nothing romantic about it. By looking at his personal relationship with Bukowski, Winans accomplishes what so few are even capable of, while most strip the flesh of the man away to reveal words. He shows how those words add up to a very complicated, caring one.

Don't let my words confuse you, A.D. Winans' **Dead Lions** is more than just a memoir and it certainly isn't some lame Wikipedia entry. This book is a clear portrait of memory, of friendship, and what we give up in the name of true independence, that not only raises the dead, but also hopefully changes how we look at their work and all of the humanity that comes along with it.

-John Dorsey
Toledo, OH- 2-26-2014

Table Of Contents

ALVAH BESSIE - June 4, 1904 – July 21, 1985

ALVAH BESSIE

Red Badge Of Courage (Are You Now Or Have You Ever Been)

Perhaps these words are not familiar to the so-called X and Y generations, but they remain imbedded in my mind. I was just a young boy when the late Senator Parnell Thomas chaired the House-An-American Activity Committee, later to be referred to as the HUAC.

I witnessed the San Francisco police turn high-pressure fire hoses on student protestors, washing them down the marble stairs, where they were dragged outside to waiting police vans. This memory is still imbedded inside my head.

Todd Lawson, a friend and cable TV host, informed me he planned to interview Alvah Bessie, one of ten persons sent to prison for refusing to testify before the HUAC and answer the question, "Are you now or have you ever been a member of the Communist Party," I asked Lawson if he would mind if I sat in on the interview, which was conducted at Lawson's small apartment in downtown San Francisco.

Today many young people are unaware of the HUAC, a Congressional Committee that resulted in the blacklisting of a sizable number of Hollywood screenwriters, directors, actors and producers, many of who would never recover from the stigma attached to their names and reputations.

Alvah Bessie and nine others refused to testify and were cited for contempt of Congress. They would become known as The Hollywood Ten.

Todd Lawson was the Director of the San Francisco Arts and Letters Foundation, and also hosted a local cable TV program. One of its purposes was to present an annual award to a deserving person in the arts. I was given the award in 1984 and Bessie received it the following year.

The interview began with cordial introductions. Prior to the interview, I went to the public library and looked up the history of Bessie. I learned he had written about his ordeal with the HUAC in a book titled *Inquisition in Eden*, an autobiographical narrative of what it had been like to work in Hollywood as a writer, to be subpoenaed, and later serve a year in prison for refusing to cooperate with the Committee. Bessie had been brought up during the Great Depression, when there was very little hope in people's lives.

Bessie and hundreds more like him traveled to Spain to fight in the Spanish Civil War, as part of the Abraham Lincoln Brigade, a fight for what they believed to be the right of the common man to govern the human condition. In 1939 Scribner's published his book *Men in Battle*, in which Bessie described his experience fighting in the Spanish Civil war.

Lawson began by asking Bessie how the HUAC came into existence. Bessie said it was important for people to remember that at the end of WW 11, our allies were not only England and France, but Russia and China too. He said there was no way we could have known they would later become our enemies.

Bessie talked about a film that was made about the National Maritime Union, which showed for the first time that American men and women were capable not only of building airplanes together but of flying them. He said this was unheard of at the time. The film portrayed women building ships, with men and women of different creeds and nationalities working in harmony with one another. Bessie said these were ideas uncommon to many Americans and considered by some in the motion picture industry to be subversive. After the war, American women were expected to return to their homes and raise their children, not to compete in the work force with men. It's no small wonder the film was seen by many as a threat to the American way of life that existed before the war.

Bessie named several well known actors like Ward Bond (Wagon Train), John Wayne (The Duke), and Adolph Menjou, who formed an organization known as "The Motion Picture Alliance For the Preservation of American Ideals," that motion picture trade unions condemned as being anti-labor, anti-union and anti-Negro.

The alliance called upon the HUAC to investigate the motion picture industry, informing the Committee that there were members of the industry who were Communists intent on destroying the American way of life.

Bessie talked about a screenwriter who also served as a critic for *Esquire* magazine who had testified before the Committee about how subtle the un-American screenwriters were, citing as an example a screenplay about a congressman giving favors to a wealthy constituent and cited this as an example of Communist propaganda. Bessie said that when the audience began laughing, the chairman of the Committee angrily pounded his gavel, and said, "There will be quiet or I'll clear the room.

The Chairman said, "Can you imagine people so low, so corrupt, so degenerate, they will show crooked congress men?"

Lawson and I broke out into laughter. Lawson said he didn't know there was anything but crooked congressmen, which brought a smile to Bessie's face.

Would that have been Senator McCarthy?" Lawson inquired.

"No, said Bessie. At this time, the Chairman was Parnell Thomas. Senator McCarthy came later.

Bessie said that Parnell Thomas had later been sent to prison along with the Hollywood Ten, after Drew Pearson, the famed newscaster, exposed him for having put several of his relatives on his Congressional payroll, family members who performed no work, but collected paychecks that were turned over to Thomas, who then deposited them in his own bank account.

Thomas pleaded No Contest and was sentenced to a prison term. Bessie grimaced as he recalled how the congressman had been given a four-year sentence, but had been pardoned by President Truman after serving but ten months of his sentence.

I told Bessie how much I admired the work of Ring Lardner and asked him if his son (Ring Lardner, Jr) had been one of the Hollywood Ten. Bessie said this was in fact the case, and that he had just purchased a beach home in Santa-Barbara, California, and was in the process of moving in when the U.S. Marshals arrived at his door with a subpoena to appear before the Committee.

"He was working for 20th Century Fox. He had won an Academy Award in 1943 for a movie starring Katherine Hepburn and Spencer Tracy. The terrible thing was not so much his going to prison, but that he was blacklisted and unable to find work for eighteen years."

Bessie said that through the entire ordeal Lardner had managed to keep a sense of humor, and that when he was called before the Committee and asked if he was or had ever been a Communist, Lardner had replied, "I could answer that question, but if I did, I would hate myself in the morning." The remark enraged the Chairman, who had Lardner thrown out of the hearings.

"I hope you won't take offense, " Lawson said, but was he or any of the others a member of the Communist Party?"

"Does it really matter?" asked Bessie. That isn't the question. It's a matter of the Constitution. We were robbed of the fundamental right of free thought. What gave the government the right to think they had the right to summon citizens before them and give an account to the government on their beliefs and their associations? Like religion, this was a matter of our own business. Lives were ruined, careers destroyed and the Industry censored, and for what?"

"I apologize for asking the question," said Lawson. "No need for that," said Bessie. "I know you don't think like that. It's just that there were powerful government people who believed that Communists had actively infiltrated the motion picture industry and these people were intent on exposing them. But they exposed nothing. The real shame is that the Supreme Court did not step in and stop what was happening until the late fifties when public opinion turned against the Committee.

Bessie talked about how un-American the Committee itself had been, refusing the accused the right to admit any writings into evidence. When Hollywood producers offered the Committee any film in the archives for the Committee to review and point out what they believed to be subversive, they were informed this was not what the Committee was there for, that the only question that mattered was "Are you now or have you ever been a member of the Communist Party."

Bessie related that the Hollywood Ten had consulted with a lawyer who said the following options were open to them: They could decide to answer the questions of the Committee and say, "I am and what about it?" Or as a group they could respond by saying, "What business is it of yours." But that if they answered in the affirmative, the next question would be about others in the industry, and if they answered they didn't know anything about these people, the Committee would produce witnesses who would say but of course they knew. Bessie and the other nine members were told by their lawyers that if they refused to answer questions, they would be cited for contempt of Congress and face a fine of up to $1.000 and a year in prison; whereas if they said anything that could be construed as perjury, they would face a fine of up to $5.000 and five years in prison. The group collectively made a decision to challenge the Committee's right to ask the question.

Among the better-known members of the Hollywood Ten sentenced to prison was Dalton Trumbo, who years later would write such acclaimed screenplays as *Spartacus* and *Exodus*.

I commended him for the group maintaining a united front. He fidgeted in his seat, paused for a moment, and said, "We stood as a team at the hearings, but one of the group later testified before the Committee."

"Who was that?" Lawson asked.

Edward Dmytryk. After he served his sentence, he went back to the Committee and testified that at one time he had been a member of the Communist Party and named five others who had been members, at the same time."

"Why do you think he did that?" Lawson wanted to know.

"Well, I believe that he said he had a change of heart, but I think it was because he wanted to go back to work. He couldn't find work, so he went before the Committee. After he testified, he had no trouble finding work."

"I don't recall any movies he was involved in," said Lawson.

"He directed *The Caine Mutiny* and *The Young Lions*. I'm sure you're aware of them," Bessie said.

Yes, of course," said Lawson. "I just didn't connect them to his name."

At this point, Bessie excused himself to visit the bathroom. When he returned, we discussed how it was for Bessie after he was released from prison and found himself blacklisted from making a living. Bessie said that like other members of the Hollywood Ten, he had been forced to live in relative obscurity, ignored by the literary establishment, who had turned their backs on him. He worked for a short time as a stage manager and soundman at Enrico Banducci's North Beach nightclub, and later managed to land a job as an editor of a union newspaper, published by Harry Bridges, who at the time was the head of the International Longshoreman's Union. A union powerful enough to disrupt and close down the San Francisco waterfront.

I told Bessie that my father had told me when I was a kid about "Bloody Thursday" (as it became known), which occurred in 1934 after the San Francisco police tried to open the docks, which were being picketed by the longshoremen. The police and picketers' clash cost the lives of two strikers and left hundreds of other people wounded. The bloody battle turned public opinion in favor of the union and made

Bridges a leading figure in the International Longshoreman's Union. Bessie replied this was but one of many things Bridges had done in the name of labor.

I asked Bessie what changed the public's mind about the HUAC. He said the man most responsible for this was Dalton Trumbo. He told us how at the 1957 Hollywood Academy Awards, Robert Rich was given an Oscar for the screenplay *The Brave One*, but when his name was called to come up on stage and receive the award, no one appeared on stage. The director of the Guild had to accept the award for him. No one had ever heard of Robert Rich. Bessie said Rich was really Dalton Trumbo, who had written the screenplay *The Brave One*, during the time he was living in Mexico after finding himself blacklisted

Bessie related that Rich was but one of several pseudo-names Trumbo used. Bessie said that Trumbo had made a mockery of both the industry and the blacklist.

"When people are given an award under other people's names, when these people don't even exist, then it becomes a comedy. Black comedy, but still comedy.

Bessie said it wasn't until eighteen years later that Trumbo received the rightful recognition for *The Brave One*.

I asked Bessie why he had gone to fight the war in Spain. He said he had been but one of more than 3,000 young men who shipped off to fight in the war, and that the Abraham Lincoln Brigade had been made up of American volunteers who fought for three years until the unit was disbanded shortly after Franco's army defeated the Republic forces on the eve of World War Two.

Bessie said there was nothing romantic about the war at all, but took pride in knowing the cause was a just one.

"I had no idea what to expect when I got there. It was advance and retreat. Dig in and move out. It was blood and gore, the fight to stay alive. I, and others like me, were drawn to the cause because the Spanish were the first to openly resist Fascism. I thought it was wrong that the U.S.

and other countries remained neutral. I never gave up hope that President Roosevelt would come around, but he never did. Look at what neutrality resulted in when it came to the Jews. There comes a point in life when you have to choose the high ground and take a moral stand.

"What was it like there?" I naively asked.

"Well, we put up a good fight and made some early headway. I mean that's pretty amazing when you consider we (volunteers) were city people. We didn't know anything about climbing mountains and digging foxholes. You're talking about university graduates and men from the trade unions and such. Some of the men were from well-to-do families. Most of us had never fired a gun."

"Do you still have memories of the country?" Lawson asked.

"Yes, of course, the country was beautiful. You remember your comrades the most. And Hemingway visited the front lines, but he could leave whenever he wanted.

I asked Bessie what kind of causalities the Brigade suffered. He replied that more than eight hundred Americans had been killed by the time the Brigade had been disbanded.

"In the end, all the foreigners were asked to pack up and leave, more than a hundred thousand men in all."

"You returned to the U.S.?" Todd asked.

"Yes, but not all of us did. Some went to France and lived in exile."

"What about today?" Lawson asked. "Who do you see as the main threat to liberty?"

"The far right," said Bessie. The people remember the sixties and the radical left, but it is the far tight who is the real danger and I don't know if the battle can be won at the ballot box."

The meeting ended all too soon, as there was so much more I wanted to talk to Bessie about. He left a lasting impression on me. Here was a man who had lived his convictions.

A man who went to prison for what he believed in. A man who fought fearlessly in the Spanish Civil War. A man whom Hemingway had openly admired. A man who had above all been a soldier and secondly a writer. The words of George Bernard Shaw came to my mind: "I have not wasted my entire life trifling with literary fools."

Bessie had stood up to the powers that be and dearly paid the price for his convictions. This is not to say he was not a talented writer, for Ernest Hemingway himself had said that Bessie's book *Men in Battle* was one of the best war novels of our time.

Later I mailed Bessie a copy of my book, *The Reagan Psalms*, a biting satire on the Reagan Administration, and told him how Studs Terkel had read portions of the book over his Chicago radio station. I hoped Bessie might comment on the book, and included in my letter, a short note telling him I had sent a copy of the book to the White House, and wanted to know if he thought I would be on a blacklist.

Bessie wrote back and said he enjoyed the book immensely. In his letter, he spoke about an incident with Scott Meredith, an agent who was in the practice of charging authors to look at their work. Bessie spoke about Meredith soliciting a manuscript from him.

"I wrote and told him I could not stand his clients, his crooked practice of demanding payment for reading one's work, or his face."

Bessie said he regretted the latter remark because it had hurt Meredith and that one could not help how they looked. He went on to relate that Meredith had told him how much he admired his "history" which Bessie said he had been surprised to hear.

Bessie proposed we hoist a drink in honor of Marilyn Monroe, who we both admired, and who Bessie had written a book about her treatment by the movie industry.

He concluded with a scathing indictment of Norman Mailer.

"That poor permanent adolescent. Let him laugh all the way to the bank. That is what he wants most."

Bessie ended by saying, "Down with all publishers and entrepreneurs except for you (If you are one) and me (Should I ever become one).

We continued to correspond with each other. In a letter written before the November elections, he responded to an earlier inquiry about my being on a literary blacklist after my public criticism of the National Endowment For the Arts Literature Program.

"You're on the list," he said. Keep firing. I notice your upside down stamp (ship in distress). SOS is coming."

In my last letter to him, I included a long anti-military poem. His reply:

"Dear Poet Laureate, your latest effort will prove to be the greatest weapon against tyranny, and chivalry, too, as Cervantes discovered, i.e. Satire. Have at him (Reagan) as hard and as often as you can and tell me how often you get your work printed by the establishment."

Bessie died in early 1985, at the age of 81. A service was held in a small chapel in Marin County. The cars that filled the parking lot were filled with old Fords and Chevy's, even an old Buick or two. The old sedans had bumper stickers that read, "End the warms race" and "U.S. out of Nicaragua."

A long line of visitors stood outside in the hot sun waiting to sign the guest book. I watched a burly and aging man help steady and older man who haltingly signed the guest book, Harry Bridges.

Two hundred-plus people gathered inside the small church to pay their last respects. The first person to eulogize Bessie was Brigade Captain Wolfe, a veteran of the Abraham Lincoln Brigade, who had earlier appeared in a documentary movie about the brigade. He spoke proudly of Bessie's many achievements and finished by saying: "He's remembered as one of the Hollywood Ten. But those of us who knew him know that he was proudest of having been a member of the Abraham Lincoln Brigade."

There were other speakers including Bessie's lawyer friend who read an excerpt from an interview with Bessie that had been conducted at the front lines in Spain. As the aging warriors filed out of the church and back into their cars, there was a sense of sadness in the air.

The old Left was coming face to face with a warrior that takes no prisoners. A warrior it could not hope to defeat, that warrior being death! Their hopes, dreams and sacrifices were facing a changing society of right wing values and open betrayals, as was the case with one of their own (Ronald Reagan) who had changed his pro-Democratic union views to take up the cause of right wing politics. Some of the more bitter ones must have been asking themselves if the fight had been worth it. Bessie himself would never have entertained that question.

At home that night I turned on my stereo and toasted a drink to the memory of Bessie. Not many writers make it to the big time and fewer still are remembered kindly by history, but Bessie had secured his place in history by standing up for his beliefs and fighting for them. How many writers can lay claim to this? How many writers have the balls that Alvah Bessie and Harry Bridges had to stand up against the establishment and fight for justice and equality for all?

JACK MICHELINE -November 6, 1929 – February 27, 1998

JACK MICHELINE

Jack Micheline, a poet of the Beat generation, died of a heart attack on February 27, 1998 aboard a transit Bart train, on his way to visit a friend in the East Bay.

Micheline was a street poet who lived on the fringe of poverty, where he was born, and later in San Francisco. He saw the Beat generation as a media fantasy that had little if anything to do with the creative spirit.

He hung out in the Greenwich Village in the early fifties, where he met Langston Hughes, the legendary Harlem poet. When Hughes was asked why he remained in Harlem, he said he preferred the company of wild men to that of wild animals. Micheline would adopt this motto as his own.

Langston Hughes was but one of many talented poets, writers and musicians whom Micheline met and associated with in the fifties while living in New York. In 1957 he received the Revolt in Literature Award. One of the presenters was the celebrated Jazz musician, Charles Mingus. This resulted in a lasting friendship between the two men, and they later performed together at San Francisco's California Music Hall. It was around this period of time Jack Kerouac wrote a foreword for Micheline's first book of Poems, *River of Red Wine*, and it was favorably reviewed in *Esquire* magazine, which further enhanced his reputation.

The fifties were an exciting time for Micheline, a period in which he met Jack Kerouac, Norman Mailer, Franz Kline, Allen Ginsberg, Gregory Corso, Herbert Gold, and other noted poets and musicians of the Beat era.

He walked the streets of his hometown writing about the down and out, the losers, and the dispossessed, and gave the word "street" poetry new meaning. He was included in Elias Wilentz's *Beat Scene* and later in Ann Charters' *Penguin Book of the Beats*.

He was born of Russian-Romanian Jewish ancestry, under the name of Harvey Martin Silver; he took to the road at a young age, working at a variety of odd jobs. It was during this time he changed his name, adopting the first name of his hero Jack London and, in part, the surname of his mother (Mitchell). He worked for a short time as a union organizer before devoting his life to poetry and painting. He was 68 years old at the time of his death, and for the last several years of his life had suffered from diabetes.

It has been said that in his younger days he had a "bad boy" persona and often took delight in his outrageous behavior. He would frequently get drunk and make coarse passes at cultured ladies. "To go into a café and go Boom! Boom! Boom! and see some woman spill coffee on her skirt is a revolution," he declared to Fielding Dawson, a New York poet friend of his.

There is little doubt that publishers like City Lights and Black Sparrow Press found his behavior offensive and probably accounts for why they never published one of the more than twenty books he published during his lifetime.

His reaction was to say, "I will never get any awards for how to win friends and influence people. I'm not a politician. I don't kiss ass. I don't play the game by the rules."

I was privileged to be his friend for more than thirty-five years. If there is such a word as "pure" he can lay claim to it, for sadly poetry has become a business world where public relations and backstabbing have become finely tuned arts, and he wanted no part of that kind of world.

He refused to bow down to anyone, choosing to write for the people: hookers, drug addicts, blue-collar workers and the dispossessed, and he did it from deep inside the heart.

He frequently boasted to me that he had never taught a creative writing class, held a residency, received a grant, or sought the favors of the "poetry business boys," whom he regarded as the enemies of poetry.

In a 1997 interview I did with him, he talked about the futility a poet faces in finding a large publisher. He said, in part:

I don't want to be published because I wear the same clothes that others wear, or because I have the same ideas. I want respect for my own individuality, but it doesn't work that way."

He didn't attend college. His university degree was the "streets" where he majored in street smarts. He wasn't concerned with semantics or the carefully arranged use of metaphors as we can see from a stanza in one of his poems.

A REAL POEM

A real poem is not in a book

It's a knockout

A long shot

A shot in the mouth

A crack of the bat

A lost midget turning into a giant

A lost soul finding its own way...

I met him in the sixties but it wasn't until the early seventies that we became close friends. It was during this time that I was editing and publishing *Second Coming,* and he became a frequent contributor to the magazine.

In 1975 *Second Coming* published a book of his poems, *Last House in America,* and in 1980 I published a small collection of his short stories, *Skinny Dynamite*.

He never received the recognition that Lawrence Ferlinghetti or the other major Beats received but the body of work he left behind is considerable and I have no doubt he will be given his rightful place in Beat History.

John Tytell, a professor at Queen's College in New York has called him a "poet of urgency and exhortation in the tradition of Jack London and Vachel Lindsey.

A self-proclaimed lyrical poet, he frequently drew on old blues and jazz rhythms, infusing the cadence of word music, while paying tribute to the gut reality of the material he wrote about. I asked him how much music influenced his poetry. His response:

"I was born to a poor family in the Bronx. I think if I had been born into a cultured family, I would have been a composer. I write the music first, not the words for it, before I write the poem. I hear the music, the rhythms, and therefore I'm basically a composer, a musician. I can't remember when music wasn't an important part of my life. Without music there is no life."

His poems ring true, because beyond the lines and stanzas flows the energy of life. His voice was an original one and no one tried to imitate it because it can't be imitated. He was truly at home with himself, and loved by both young and old alike. Although he exasperated many people with his outspokenness, his true friends saw through this facade, and paid attention to his love for the common man and woman.

In my interview with him, he said: "I never wanted to be a poet. I still don't want to be a poet. I just want to live my life. The thing is people don't understand poetry. All they have is their football, baseball, and television. They've never had a chance to see a real poet that relates to them.

"What they need are poems that relate to their own way of life. In America, everything is profit motivation.

"It's the spirit that I relate to. The church doesn't do the job. Television doesn't do the job. Everything in America is based on greed, money and mediocrity."

Ignored by the poetry establishment and the larger alternative presses, he went about his writing, fighting off the disillusionment and bitterness that have overcome so many poets his age.

His poems were from his heart and years of personal experience on the streets. Poems that were questioning and probing, and often accusing, but always rang out with truth and conviction.

At the age of twelve, he happened upon a copy of *Studs Lonigan*, and found eerie comparisons to what he read in the book and in the cruelty and injustice he saw in the streets he was raised on. However, convinced that poets were "sissies", he didn't take up writing until the age of twenty-four. When he did begin writing, it was with a desire to find poetry in the everyday happenings of life. He sensed true poets don't choose poetry, but that poetry chooses them, and that in the end it's the way you live your life that counts.

Walking the streets of Harlem and the Village, he inherited the richness of the culture, especially the culture of black musicians. He found himself drawn to the warmth and humor of the black musicians and poets he encountered in the after hour jazz clubs, and quickly became a major figure in the fifties Greenwich Village Beat scene.

He identified himself with the street poet Maxwell Bodenheim, and early on struck up a friendship with Eddie Balchowsky, who had lost his arm in the Spanish War, but who had gone on to become a respected visual artist.

Balchowsky walked him through the alleys of New York, pointing out things Micheline had not noticed before.

"Balchowsky gave me my eyes," said Micheline. He explained that Balchowsky had emphasized, "Before you can see, you must first rid yourself of the misconceptions that ordinary people accept without question.

Micheline described Greenwich Village as a poor, working class Italian neighborhood, where rent was cheap, and the people poor, but the center of artistic expression, where people were at ease relating to one another.

Tired of the New York Village scene, he left in the early sixties for California and adopted San Francisco as his new home.

It didn't take him long before he became a force in the North Beach literary community:

"Poetry was everywhere. Every day Kaufman and I read a poem. It isn't part of history, but I was arrested for pissing on a police car the same night Kaufman was arrested outside the Co-Existence Bagel Shop. We were taken down to the Kearney Street police station and thrown in the drunk tank, where both of us were beaten."

If he screamed poet loud and often, perhaps it was because the literary establishment unfairly ignored him.

He did, however, achieve his fifteen minutes of fame when in his later years he appeared on the *Late Night with Conan O'Brien, show,* where he read a poem accompanied on the trumpet by his long time friend, Bob Feldman.

We don't know much about his years growing up as a child. We do know he was born premature; a six-month, two-pound six-ounce baby, who had to fight for survival, even as he did in later life. By his own admission, he described himself as a "shy and dreamy" boy who grew up in the poor section of the Bronx, born to parents who fought like "cats and dogs."

In his writings, he describes his mother as a religious woman, who cried a lot, but who possessed a heart of gold. He paints a portrait of his father as a bitter postal worker who seldom smiled after losing everything he owned in the 1929 stock market crash.

He said as a kid he felt lost in crowds, and preferred to walk the streets alone, looking at the neighborhood lights, or walking to the Bronx Park, which was miles away from where he lived. It was here at the park that he was able to find a semblance of peace, a welcome relief from the constant bickering of his parent. He said of those early years:

I always seemed to be on edge, nervous and self conscious."

He was forced by his mother to regularly go to the synagogue and take Hebrew lessons. Carrying his Hebrew books under his arms on his way home from school, he often had to defend himself from bully Catholic boys lying in wait for him.

He said, "It was not easy being a Jew. I did not know what to believe, or who to believe in. I did not know my mother, brother, or my father. No one seemed real. It was as if everyone was acting a part in a play.

In a short story, he talks about coming home after receiving a beating by neighborhood bullies, and how his mother tended to his wounds and tried to console him.

"I went to my room and cried. Tears and torment poured out of my head. It was a hell of a world. There had to be a place somewhere where it wasn't hell, where fear didn't choke you like a knife, where you wouldn't have to hide in your own skin, and swear at the Bastard earth."

In search of that elusive peace, he began a long trek across America; recording in his notebook everything he saw and heard, even at the age of seventeen serving a stint in the Army Medical Corps. By the time he was nineteen, he found himself in Israel. Then it was back to the United States where he worked at a variety of odd jobs while traveling Kerouac's *On the Road*.

He spent a short time in Chicago, writing from a cheap $6-a-week hotel room, and described himself as a possessed man, who slept little, as he wandered the streets at all hours," mumbling to myself and counting empty beer cans." But his best creative years were in Greenwich Village and San Francisco's North Beach.

He saw the poet as a revolutionary whose purpose in life was to free people from the slavery of stifling jobs and relationships. He believed it was the poet's job to live poems and set a fearless example for others. He was a close friend of the late Charles Bukowski (Hank) in the days before Hank became famous.

They drank together at Hank's pad, and he recalled to me how John Martin (Black Sparrow Press) would come over to Hank's apartment and leave him art supplies so that Hank could create drawings, which he used to promote his books.

"We became good friends," said Micheline. We went to the track together, a few times. He was very vulnerable, but he changed, like everyone does after they become famous. He had to protect himself. That's understandable. He had a magic there, and it carried over to his writing."

The love relationship between them is evident from a July 16, 1973 letter that Hank wrote me:

"Micheline is all right---he's one-third bull shit, but he's got a special divinity and a special strength. He's got perhaps a little too much of a POET sign pasted to his forehead, but more often than not he says the good things --in speech and poem --power- flame, laughing things. I like the way his poems roll and flow. His poems are total feelings beating their heads on barroom floors.

"I can't think of anyone who has more and who has been neglected more. Jack is the last of the holy preachers sailing down Broadway singing the song. Going over all the people I've ever known, he comes closer to the utmost divinity, the soothsayer, the gambler, the burning of stinking buckskin than any man I've ever known."

Their friendship transcended their different view-points on poetry. Micheline saw poetry as a holy message that was intended for the masses while Bukowski saw it as just another job, no different from a carpenter or a plumber, and certainly nothing holy about it. Micheline read for the pure love of it while Bukowski read for a paid audience.

In his youth, he was by his own admission a wild man. One night in New York, after leaving a literary party, he found himself dancing up West 8ᵗʰ Street, on his way to the Cedar Tavern, when two cops tried to place him under arrest for being drunk and disorderly. He wrestled the two officers to the ground, suffering cuts and bruises, and in the process, bit one of the officer's on the nose. He was taken to a nearby hospital emergency room, and a doctor who by chance had heard him read his poems at a local club attended to his wounds. The doctor told the officers that while he was drunk that he was otherwise okay. The two officers disagreed and took him to Bellevue Hospital where he was admitted to the psychiatric wing on a seventy-two hour hold.

In one of his short stories, he recalls Ward Nine of the psychiatric wing as a home for the damned. "The smell of antiseptic prevailed. Everyone was shot up with drugs."

There is no denying he found a wealth of writing from his short jail incarcerations and short stay at the mental ward. He recalls a man named Doc, who from a wheelchair made regular rounds on the ward, and a tall, skinny patient named Moe who lovingly played an imaginary saxophone. These were the kind of people who became the subject matter of his poems. On his release from Bellevue, he walked the streets back down to the East side, spitting into the darkness of death, vowing that life has to encourage more life.

"I drank, wept, and pissed and created in the darkness of a world which seemed bent on destroying itself through its ignorance, fear, greed, and insensitivity and futility of its existence."

After moving from New York to San Francisco, he was again arrested, this time by the San Francisco Police, outside the Co-Existence Bagel Shop, and charged with indecent exposure, for pissing in public. He was taken to the Hall of Justice and forced to spend the night in the drunk tank.

The next morning he appeared before the judge and listened to the charges being read: "Urinating on the corner of Grant and Green." When he showed no shame, the judge became outraged, and ordered him sent to County Hospital for mental observation. When he next appeared before the judge, he said he swallowed his pride and apologized to the judge, who gave him a ten-day suspended sentence.

He remained a wild man well into the 1980s, when he became ill with diabetes, and was forced to give up drinking. The wild times became but blurred memories, like the time he visited Hank in Los Angeles, arriving unannounced at Hank's apartment, carrying with him a stack of paintings and poems. After a day at the races and a night of drinking, Hank told him he could sleep overnight, and offered him his living room sofa. According to Hank, he sensed that Micheline might vomit, and placed a wastebasket near his head. He told him if he had to vomit, to hit the wastebasket.

Hank said the following morning he got up and drove Micheline to the airport to catch his airplane back to San Francisco. On returning home, he discovered Micheline had vomited, had completely missed the wastebasket, and had wiped up the mess with a magazine Hank had been published in.

It was incidents like this that cost him more than a few friendships, but his real friends found it hard to stay angry with him. While there is no denying he was sometimes loud and abrasive, it is also true that what he said was honest, even if sometimes blunt and brutal. If one could get past his some times abrasive personality, they found he was a force to be reckoned with.

It had to have hurt him not to receive the recognition afforded peers like Ferlinghetti, Corso, and McClure, and he didn't make it any easier on himself by offending those in a position to help him.

In his last years his fight with diabetes had taken a toll on him. He looked all his age and then some, but he was still indomitable, giving readings and presenting art shows throughout the city.

Sharing a cup of coffee with him a few short months before his death, I looked out the window of the café and saw two punk rockers walking by. It reminded me of the time a group of punk rockers came to one of his readings, intent on hooting him down, but who in the end found themselves wildly applauding him. No one could win over an audience the way Micheline could. He lived by the credo that to be a poet in America is to be an outlaw. His poems were his six guns, never backing down from anyone or any-thing. From a poem of his:

The steps move the heart

The heart fuels the eye

The mirror of the brain

Listen to the rhythm of your breath

This is how rare poems are written

Not with words but with strange notes

That moves the pen on the page

This is the eye of the storm

The earthquake

God's gift to nature

Immortality.

I'm proud to have been his friend for thirty years. To have broke bread with him, to have gotten drunk with him, to have laughed and cried with him. There is and was no closer a friend.

Shortly after his death I submitted a proposal to the San Francisco Board of Supervisors to rename a street in North Beach after him. On November 18, 2003, the City of San Francisco honored him by renaming an alley in North Beach after him. He now joins such noted Beat poets and writers as Bob Kaufman, Lawrence Ferlinghetti, Kenneth Rexroth, and Jack Kerouac, whose names adorn North Beach streets and alleys.

BOB KAUFMAN - April 18, 1925 – January 12, 1986

BOB KAUFMAN

Bob Kaufman, known in France as the "American Rimbaud," was one of the original Beat poets to come out of the fifties. He is considered by many to be the equal of any of the Beat poets, including Allen Ginsberg.

His poems are filled with the infusion of Jazz, and in North Beach, the home of the West Coast Beats, he was known as the be-bop poet.

In the fifties Kaufman co-edited *Beatitude Magazine* with fellow poet William Margolis, while reading his work with the likes of Allen Ginsberg, Lawrence Ferlinghetti, Michael McClure, Diane di Prima, and other noted poets.

In North Beach, in a six-block area from lower Grant Avenue to upper Grant Avenue, there existed a large number of bars, cafes, and coffee houses frequented by poets, artists, and jazz musicians. While Grant Avenue was the center stage of creativity, the bevy of coffee houses and bars extended from Broadway and Columbus, all the way down to the produce district where "Big Daddy Nord held court. Bob Kaufman and his wife Eileen were frequent participants in the rowdy activities that ultimately drew the attention of the police.

Kaufman seldom talked about his childhood and upbringing in New Orleans, but we know from Eileen Kaufman that he was the youngest of thirteen children, born on April 18, 1925, the son of an Orthodox Jew and a Negress from Martinique. His grandmother came to the U.S. on a slave ship from the gold coast and he was deeply proud of his African roots.

As a child, his mother saw to it that he regularly attended Catholic mass, but he also joined his father in the synagogue, on the Sabbath, while at the same time learning about the voodoo beliefs of his grandmother.

Kaufman's religious upbringing was nothing less than a spiritual mosaic, although in later life he would mock God in several of his poems.

Kaufman was arguably the most intelligent of all the Beat poets and writers, including Ginsberg. He boarded a ship at a young age, and for twenty years sailed with the U.S. Merchant Marines, traveling around the world several times. It was during one of these trips to Greenland that he suffered frostbite that caused him to lose forty percent of his hearing.

His literary education began at sea when a first-mate introduced him to the work of Jack London.

His formal education was at an elementary school in New Orleans. He would later attend the New School of Social Research in New York City, where he met Allen Ginsberg and William Burroughs. He would not meet Allen Ginsberg and Neil Cassady until he moved to California in 1958.

In May 1958 Kaufman met a young woman named Eileen, and a short time later they were married.

In 1958 City Lights published his first broadside *Abomunist Manifesto* and a second broadside, *Second April* In 1959, City Lights published a third broadside *Does the Secret Mind Whisper*. These broadsides earned Kaufman a cult following in San Francisco's North Beach district.

In the early part of 1959, Ron Rice directed a film titled *The Flower Thief*, which was shot in San Francisco, starring the North Beach bohemians, with Kaufman playing a leading role The film was later shown in Italy, where it received critical acclaim.

In late 1959, and into the early part of 1960, Kenneth Tynam produced a film titled *Dissent in the Arts in America*. Kaufman appeared in the film, which was never shown in the

U.S., after Tynam was called to appear before the infamous HUAC The film was, however, shown in Europe and helped Kaufman obtain popularity abroad.

In the early sixties he read his poetry at places like the Gaslight, and other popular Greenwich Village places, but in 1963 returned to San Francisco.

On a November 1963 afternoon, Kaufman would witness the assassination of JFK and took a Buddhist vow of silence that lasted nearly twelve years, until the end of the Vietnam War. This is only partly true, for Kaufman did on occasion speak with friends, even if only to say hello or to bum a cigarette.

Kaufman was not a prolific writer, but his poetry books are generally regarded as among the best verse written by any of the Beat poets. His first book, *Solitudes Crowded with Loneliness,* was published in 1965 by New Directions, and caused an immediate stir in local literary circles.

The book consisted mainly of early poems written while he traveled from New York to San Francisco and back again. It would later be published in France, in 1975, and help him gain a larger foreign audience. Kaufman's second book, *The Golden Sardine,* was published in 1967 by City Lights Publishing House, and earned him a solid reputation in the U.S., England, and France.

By the late fifties, Ginsberg, Corso, and the rest of the Beat gang had left North Beach, leaving behind Lawrence Ferlinghetti to tend City Lights Bookstore.

Other than Ferlinghetti, Kaufman was the last of the recognized original gang of Beats to regularly make the rounds of North Beach.

Kaufman would not see another book of his in print until 1981 when New Directions published *Ancient Rain,* which consisted of previously published poems alongside unpublished poems written between the years of 1973 and 1978.

Kaufman emerged from near obscurity in 1982, when he appeared on the PBS television show (*Images,*), but from that time on would only occasionally read his work at local literary events.

Jack Micheline, a Beat poet friend of Kaufman, said in an interview I did with him that he considered Kaufman to be a true jazz poet, a poet deeply steeped in the tradition of jazz. His work is essentially improvisational, and was at its best when accompanied by jazz.

His poetic technique resembles that of the surreal school of poets, ranging from a powerful lyrical vision to a more prophetic tone that can be found in his political poems.

Golden Sardines contains a striking political poem on the death of Caryl Chessman, a convicted kidnapper, robber, and accused rapist, who many even today feel was wrongly sentenced to death for a crime (kidnap and rape) of which he was innocent. The tone of the poem is one of anger against a system intent on destroying the mind and body. Kaufman's defiance parallels Chessman's own defiance, evidenced by Chessman refusing to admit his guilt and be spared the gas chamber.

Carl (sic) Chessman knows the Governor of

California knows. Good Johnny the Pope

Knows, Salvatore Agron knows & all the

Leaky eyed poets know. In their poems

No one is guilty of any thing at any time

Anywhere in any place

The difference between Kaufman's anger and the anger expressed by other Beat poets is that he could move from anger to humor in a matter of seconds. But even within the humor we find a biting message of condemnation of what the poet considered a system speaking of honor and God on the one hand and practicing rape and plunder on the other.

His work was frequently laced with comments on death; his obsession, perhaps awe, with death is evident in such early poems as "Results of A Lie Detector Test," which first appeared in *The Golden Sardine*.

From the sleeping calendar I have stolen a

month

I am afraid to look at it. I don't want to know

its name

Clenched in my fist I feel its frost. Its icy

face.

I cannot face the bewildered summer with a

pocketful of snow

I imagine the accusing finger of children

who will never be born

How to shut out the cries of the suffering

Death wishers, awaiting

The silent doors of winter tombs, deprived of

cherished exits.

I shall never again steal a month...

or a week

or a day or an hour

Or a minute, or a second, unless I become

desperate again.

      You won't find any pretension in Kaufman's poems. There is no attempt at word play. The poems fall naturally without a hint of strain to them. His early poems still ring true today, even after more than two decades have passed-by. A clear indicator of his power as a poet.

      Kaufman also spoke of a driving force of love. Many of his poems speak of dreams and the imagery the mind produces, as if the poet realizes it is the dream that keeps the artist going.

      But Kaufman saw through the dream as evidenced in his poem, *The Golden Sardine,* "The Mind For All Its Reasoning."

The mind for all its complicated reasoning

Is dependent on the whim of the eyelid

The most nonchalant of human parts

Opening and closing at random

Spending its hours in mystique

Filled with memories of glimpses

& blinks.

      His work is particularly harsh toward the church. In "Early Loves," he closes his poem with 'Tears will wash away her dirty murdered soul/God will be called upon to atone for his sins."

I live alone, like a pith in a tree

My teeth rattle, like musical instruments

In one ear a spider spins its web of eyes

In the other a cricket chirps all night

This is the end

Which are, that proves my glory has brought

me

I would die for poetry.

To have the privilege of reading his work, sharing a drink with him, or to have read with him, and spent time with him in his small North Beach hotel room, with little or no conversation, was an experience not easily forgotten.

Kaufman considered himself a Buddhist and believed that a poet had a call to a higher order. Like the Buddhist he accepted a vow of poverty and a non-materialistic life. He wasn't like many of the Beat poets who frequented the beach in that he never attempted to push his own literary career. He was an oral poet who didn't write for publication or expectations of fame and fortune, which is what drew me to him.

When I returned home from the military in 1958, North Beach was where it was happening. It was poetry, music, and the spoken word. Jazz was central to what was happening. Wes Montgomery and Cal Tjader were very much part of the scene. The Fillmore district, a largely black community, was known as "Bop City," a hangout for musicians like Ella Fitzgerald and Sarah Vaughan, and other jazz notables. It was not unusual to see New York jazz musicians visiting San Francisco's Fillmore district, and it was here that musicians and lovers of jazz music gathered in the early hours of the morning. Poets like Kaufman fed off the vibrations.

Kaufman soon became the undisputed street poet who frequented the Co-Existence Bagel Shop located on the corner of Grant and Green, writing and reciting his poetry there. He also liked to frequent Aquatic Park during the early morning hours, after the bars had closed down.

I frequently saw him in the company of two black male friends; Kaufman and one of the other two scribbling down their thoughts on paper, while the third member played the conga drums, passing around a bottle of red wine, or lighting up a stick of weed. They would still be there when I left for home in the wee hours of the morning.

It wasn't that poets had not been in the area long before the Beat poets arrived. It was just that for the most part they were largely invisible, while the jazz scene, on the other hand, flourished. Then along came Lenny Bruce, whose comedy routine at the time was considered outrageous and obscene. Bruce no doubt inspired others to come out and say what was on their minds, even if it meant being arrested, as Bruce frequently was. Not that Bruce didn't encourage the police, seemingly taking delight in baiting them, waiting for the right moment to drop the word "cocksucker" on them, bringing a quick close to the show. In this, he and Kaufman had something in common, when it came to taunting the police.

Kaufman's nights at the Co-Existence Bagel Shop are legendary with North Beach regulars who remember his bouts with police officer William Bigarani. I went to high school with officer Bigarani. I knew him to be a bully, and suspected he was a racist. It had to gall him to see Kaufman with a white woman. Never one to back down from a confrontation, it didn't take long for Kaufman to become a marked man. He frequently found himself hauled down to the old Hall of Justice, where he was introduced to a cop's alter ego, the nightstick.

To be fair, the San Francisco Police were fairly permissive in their attitude toward the Beats, at least until the area began to be overrun with college students looking for cheap thrills and the usual tourist crowd.

The truth is that Kaufman often encouraged the wrath of the police, seemingly goading them on to a confrontation. He considered the Bagel Shop to be his private domain.

I often hung out at the Bagel Shop and vividly recall Kaufman entering the establishment, climbing up on top of one of the tables, and reciting a newly written poem. Indeed some people hung out at the Co-Existence Bagel Shop in the hope of seeing him come in and read his work. The audience hung on his every word. But his fate was sealed the day he wrote on the walls of the Co-Existence Bagel Shop, "Adolph Hitler, growing tired of fooling around with Eve Braun, and burning Jews, moved to San Francisco and became a cop." This was the beginning of Kaufman regularly being hauled down to City Prison, to spend the night, before facing a stern-faced judge in the morning.

In 1978 Kaufman abruptly renounced writing and again withdrew into solitude, not emerging again until 1982, to read one of his poems on the PBS television show *Images*. From 1980 up until the time of his death, he would occasionally read his poems in public, but by then he had been reduced to a ghost of his former self, walking the streets of North Beach, a twitching, blinking mostly un-speaking victim of a failing liver, and a brain diminished by drugs and forced shock treatments undergone earlier at Bellevue Hospital.

The last five years of his life saw him banned from every bar in North Beach except the Camel's Club, across the street from the old Co-Existence Bagel Shop. It was only here and in Chinatown that he could go to enjoy a drink and cigarette. But the Kaufman of the eighties was a tired Kaufman. As early as 1965, he wrote, "My body is a torn mattress/disheveled throbbing place/for the comings and goings/of loveless transients/before completely objective mirrors/I have shot myself with my eyes/but death refused my advances."

Kaufman had a magical way of appearing from out of the blue. I'd be sitting at a bar having a drink when from out of nowhere, he would appear, asking for a cigarette or reciting the poems of Pound, Eliot and Blake.

Kaufman was a great influence on me. I recall one evening in the sixties, I was standing alone in the back of the Coffee Gallery, during an open "mic" poetry reading, when suddenly from behind, I felt a hand on my shoulder It was Kaufman.

"Are you going to read your work tonight?" He asked me. I hadn't planned on reading that night, and told him I had not brought any poems with me. He looked me in the eye and said, "I came to hear you read."

I left the bar and drove several miles across town in a driving rainstorm to pick up some poems at my apartment. Convinced he would be gone by the time I returned to the Coffee Gallery, I found him sitting alone at the back of the room, seemingly caught up in a private conversation with himself. I read several poems that evening, very much aware of his eyes on me, and finished the reading by dedicating the last poem to him. When I finished the poem, I looked over at the table, and saw he had left the bar as quietly as he had appeared.

Until that evening I had been reluctant to read in public, and I believe he must have sensed my insecurity. From that night on, I became a regular reader at the Coffee Gallery, and had Kaufman to thank for helping me overcome my fear of reading in public, a phobia that followed me from grammar school into adulthood.

Kaufman's humor showed not only in his poetry, but in his life as well. I recall the time he walked into the Coffee Gallery (now the Lost and Found bar), where Gregory Corso was holding court in the back of the bar, enjoying the admiration of a group of young admirers. A young woman challenged Corso to name the major poets of his era, and

Corso began rattling off several names, which not surprisingly included his own. He identified Kaufman and Micheline as minor poets. He was unaware Kaufman had entered the bar and was standing near the doorway. I turned in his direction and asked him where he would rate Corso. Without hesitation, he smiled and said, "Major Minor," leaving the bar to loud applause.

I recall yet another time at the Vesuvio Bar, located adjacent to City Lights, when a tourist guide bus double-parked outside the bar to allow passengers to debark and use the establishment's restroom.

As the small group of middle-aged tourists departed the bus and made their way into the bar, the tour guide began his rehearsed speech:

"This is where the Beat Generation began."

Suddenly Kaufman jumped up on one of the tables, and shouted in a loud voice: "No. No. Alice Toklas was commissioned by the Pope to do a book, and Gertrude Stein jumped out of the looking glass, and declared it the Beat age." The tourists quickly exited the bar, no doubt thinking Kaufman a mad man.

I had a special place in my heart for Kaufman. There was something mystical about him. I recall a night in the seventies when I was stoned out of my mind on drugs and "Jack Daniels," a suicidal combination. I staggered down Green Street on my way to Gino and Carlo's bar when from out of the shadows of a closed pizza place, a shadow jumped out at me. It was Kaufman dressed in a Mexican poncho.

He reached out and firmly grabbed my arm. Before I could say a word, he said in a soft voice, "A.D., Crazy John, a great book." Then just as suddenly he disappeared down the street. He was referring to a recently published book of mine, *The Further Adventures of Crazy John,* which I had given him a year earlier. It was a surreal experience I've never forgotten. The next day I began work on a long prose poem ("America"), which is one of the strongest political poems I have written. I would later read the poem at a benefit reading for Kaufman, held at the Little Fox Theater, to a crowd of over 300 people. Kaufman's smile contributed to one of the strongest readings I have given.

The night Kaufman is said to have officially broken his vow of silence, I was sitting at Spec's bar in North Beach when he again appeared from out of nowhere. I watched him eye the crowd, many of whom were waiting to go to a party being hosted by Miriam Patchen. Within moments of his entrance, Kaufman launched into a spontaneous recitation from the works of T.S. Eliot, William Blake, and Ezra Pound. Despite the drugs and past forced shock treatments, he was still able to recite the old masters from memory. I sat there watching the veins on his neck stand out with each poem he read.

This was to be Kaufman's last hurrah, although there would be benefit readings, like the 1977 Street Poets reading, which I organized at the University of California Extension Center. The reading featured Kaufman, Jack Micheline and myself. Kaufman was a twitching ball of nervous energy the day of the reading. In order to make sure he would show up for the reading, it was necessary for me to pick him up in North Beach and literally baby-sit him those long hours before the reading.

We were having a cup of coffee at a nearby coffee shop when he began mumbling something about La Guna Honda, a county hospital and old age home. I had a cousin who had been forced to spend her last days there, and knew what a depressing institution it was. I was aware that a friend of Kaufman's had recently been hospitalized there. With hours to spare before the reading and tired of the coffee shop, I on the spur of the moment, decided to drive to the hospital. The grounds themselves are quite beautiful, unlike the inside of the institution.

I parked the car at the lower end of the grounds, and shut the engine off, when suddenly Kaufman began reciting "The Love Song of J. Alfred Prufrock." I believe he was paying a final tribute to his friend. (George). Afterwards we drove back to the coffee shop and found ourselves joined at the table by Eileen Kaufman.

She was excited about the reading and had brought a tape recorder with her. Several times Kaufman looked anxiously from Eileen to me.

"Don't give Eileen the money. You pay me," he blurted out. He repeated this sentiment several times until I assured him I would pay him and not Eileen. In fairness to Eileen, she was only looking after his interest, knowing that after the reading he would return to North Beach and spend the money on his drinking friends, but I felt it was his money to spend as he wished.

Back then North Beach regulars were a funny lot, seldom leaving the safety of their neighborhood, but for this special occasion they came in great numbers to hear his magic one more time. He didn't disappoint them. He stepped up on stage to loud applause, and almost instantly I realized he was revising his poems on stage. This is a remarkable feat, especially for someone in the condition he was in.

The one thing I was able to accomplish for Kaufman was to assist him in obtaining an NEA writing grant. In the seventies, at the height of my publishing success, I was on good terms with Leonard Randolph, the Director of the NEA Literature Program. It didn't matter what the grants panel voted on, if Randolph wanted you to receive a grant, it was a done deal. I knew this was the case when I approached him and told him that Kaufman deserved an NEA grant.

I considered done when Randolph turned to me and said, "Have someone fill out and submit the grant application." I have since heard that others claim credit for Kaufman receiving the grant, and that's fine with me. The truth is Kaufman deserved the grant, strictly on the merits of his work and not the influence of others.

Lynne Wildey gave Kaufman shelter and comfort in the last years of his life. I never saw him much the last two years of his life, after he moved out of North Beach. Being the warrior he was, he fought off the advances of Lady Death until January 12, 1986.

`I was in North Beach celebrating my fiftieth birthday when Shig Muro, the Manager of City Lights, stopped me on the street to tell me that Kaufman had died at the age of sixty from emphysema and a failed liver.

My first reaction was one of shock, then rage. Again the heavy hand of death had come to claim another victim. I found myself walking from bar to bar, informing first one and then another person of Kaufman's death. The inevitable "shit" followed the reaction or "God Damn." The truth is that death is not a good conversationalist.

As I walked down the street to the Vesuvio bar, I recalled the last time Kaufman and I had drank together at North Beach. We were sitting at a bar in Chinatown when he asked me if I owned a radio. When I replied that I did, he looked at me, and said, "You can listen to jazz." Not a surprising statement, for jazz was a big part of Kaufman's life. He knew many of the great jazz musicians and his poetry was literally filled with jazz.

Kaufman will be duly recorded by "Beat" historians (and honored as he was in the Whitney Museum Beat Art Exhibit), and rightfully so. The shame is that his Beat peers, caught up in their own egomania, made little effort to see he gained the full recognition he deserved.

Kaufman had told me earlier, "Death is hunting me down." On Sunday, January 12, 1986, the hunt ended.

On Friday, January 17, 1986, they came from all over - 250 poets and friends - to pay their last respects to perhaps the most prominent black Beat poet of our time. The predominately white background faced a black priest and jazz group at Sacred Heart Church in San Francisco, near the black Fillmore district. Ferlinghetti read a letter from Allen Ginsberg, who was in New York and unable to attend the memorial. Michael McClure read a poem by Kaufman

I thought it odd seeing Kaufman eulogized inside a church since he was an acknowledged atheist, and the lines from one of his poems came to mind: God you're just an empty refrigerator/with a dead child

I was moved by Micheline reading a poem for his friend to a large gathering outside the church, while a city bus passed by with passengers peering out the windows.

I don't think Kaufman would have minded the church service. He might even have been amused by it.

At noon, a crowd of over a hundred mourners met at the Mirage Bar on Guerrero Street for a sharing of memories that lasted well into the evening. At 10 p.m., Kaufman's son (parker) and I went to dinner with a mutual friend for a final sharing of memories.

Kaufman's ashes were scattered at sea on Thursday, January 23, 1986, according to his wishes. Earlier a jazz procession made its way up Grant Avenue, stopping to play music at each of the bars Kaufman had once drank at.

Kaufman maintained his sense of humor right up until the end. Lynne Wildey told me how she had visited him shortly before his death. She said as she was preparing to leave, Kaufman looked up at her, smiled, and said, "Stop by the next time you're in the neighborhood."

The Beats had lost one of their proudest warriors. If Tony Bennett left his heart in San Francisco, Kaufman left his in the streets of North Beach.

SECOND COMING ANTHOLOGY

Ten Years in Retrospect

CHARLES BUKOWSKI - August 16, 1920 – March 9, 1994

CHARLES BUKOWSKI

Charles Bukowski (known to his friends as Hank) and I were friends for over seventeen years. We became friends in 1973 when I was editing and publishing *Second Coming* magazine/press, and continued our friendship over the long years. In 1974 we became particularly close after I published a Special *Second Coming* Bukowski issue.

In letters, in telephone conversations, and in personal meetings, Hank and I discussed the small press world and the role the poet has played in its development and history.

Hank spent decades writing for the small magazines before he was an established and financial success. It' been two decades since his death and his books are still being sold worldwide.

There are people who believe you have to break bread or drink with a person on an on-going basis before you can call that person a friend. I don't subscribe to this point of view. I never met the late William Wantling, arguably one of the best poets to graduate from the U.S. penal system, but we corresponded regularly up until the time of his death and I considered him a close friend.

I only met Hank a few times, but he too was a friend of mine. At a low point in my life, when friends are needed the most, he wrote and said:

"I know that you are down and out, low on coin, and spiritually molested like the rest of us, with little chance but to hang on by the fingernails, work a line or two down on paper, walk down the street and breathe in the air of this shit life we put upon ourselves."

This statement says a lot about who Hank was. He was a man who shot straight from the hip, the same way I have tried to do my entire life. There was no game playing between us. No need to wear masks. We accepted each other for what we were, warts and all.

Hank was not a hero, as many people have tried to make him out to be. He was like all of us, a man possessed with both good and bad traits. As he told me, at the home of Linda King, "I haven't yet met a saint I like." He wasn't the personification of Jesus, or the reincarnation of Satan. He was simply put, a damn fine poet and writer, but there is more to life than writing about whores, pimps, drunks and Sunday morning hangovers.

Hank was a man of many virtues and admirable qualities, but to see him (as many do) as the Robin Hood of literature, a man whose motives and actions are in the best interest of the down and out, simply ignores the fact he betrayed and tore apart many former friends, both in short stories and in vindictive poems, frequently breaking off friendships whenever someone got too close to him, and often on brutal terms. As the late Marvin Malone and I learned, the less personal contact you had with him, the more he respected you, and the fewer attacks you faced.

It's possible his inability to deal with love was the result of an unhappy childhood. He suffered from a skin condition resulting in disfiguring boils that left his face a road map of scars, and because of this, he often found himself cruelly taunted by his peers.

At home, he received little comfort, and often found himself subjected to beatings by an ill-tempered and abusive father who, when he wasn't beating his son, often took out his anger on his wife.

If a person has never known true love in his life, it can be a frightening experience, for love requires trust, and I don't think Hank trusted many people. There are many documented examples of his turning against former friends.

I myself would suffer the very same fate, but the fact remains Hank was an important part of *Second Coming*. He represented what *Second Coming* was all about.

I have yet to meet another poet or writer who had the talent Hank had. To be sure, there were many bad poems and short stories that should never have seen print, but what writer among us can truthfully say he or she hasn't suffered the same fate?

No one moved me as deeply as Hank or had the ability to bring tears to my eyes as Hank did in his "Poem For Jane," and let there be no doubt he had few rivals when it came to humor.

His first book, *Post Office,* was written in nineteen days. The book is filled with laughter that shines through the pain of working at a dead-end job that kills a man's spirit and physically breaks him down. I know! I worked for the San Francisco post office for over five years, some of the very same years Hank was employed at the Los Angeles post office.

On his death, he left behind a body of unpublished poems and short stories that are still being published today, assuring his legion of fans he will be with us for years to come.

It was March 1994, and I was reading the newspaper in my apartment when I turned to the entertainment section on the San Francisco Chronicle and was shocked to find the obituary of Charles Bukowski.

I found it odd to find an obituary in the entertainment section of a newspaper, but in retrospect, there was nothing odd about it at all Hank had carefully scripted his reputation as a hard drinking, womanizing hero of the unfortunate and the downtrodden, the same people who bought his books and identified so strongly with him.

In the end, he became as much an entertainer as he was a poet and a writer. This is evidenced by the fact that in his last years, the actor Sean Penn became one of his closest friends. Entertainer or not, I was stunned to learn Hank was dead at the age of seventy-three.

Hank is on record as saying he never expected to live

a long life. It's also a matter of record that in his mid-thirties, he lay near death from a bleeding ulcer in a Los Angeles hospital charity ward, the direct result of too many years of heavy drinking.

I had been aware for some time he was battling a series of ailments brought on by advanced age and abuse of his body, but had not dwelled much on the matter. Most people tend to avoid thinking about death until it stares them straight in the face, as if not thinking about it will delay the inevitable outcome.

In reality, death was a re-occurring theme in many of Hank's poems, especially over the last several years of his life. And it stalked his mythical character in his final novel (*Pulp*) published shortly before his death.

I was saddened we had not corresponded with each other for several years. He was angered over a poem I wrote, which I don't believe was a put-down poem (Small Press Poet Makes It Big). At the time I felt he might even find it humorous, given the fact he had poked fun at so many poets and writers over the long years.

I may not even have written the poem had he not told me early on in our friendship that one day I would read about him going cat fishing with James Dickey and Norman Mailer and when that day came, I could write about it and he would understand. However, it was not Dickey or Mailer who inspired me to write the poem, as much as it was the presence of actor Sean Penn and other Hollywood luminaries who came into his life after he gained a measure of fame.

Even in his wildest dreams, he would never have imagined that some day he would have Hollywood idols paying him homage and coming to his home, brining with them what Hank said were God Awful poems.

Bukowski had a long history of turning on once close friends of his. One of those friends was John Bryan, a fringe member of the Beat generation. Bryan was the former editor and publisher of *Open City,* who first paid Bukowski for his column "Notes From A Dirty Old Man" The lengthy list includes well-known small press figures Harold Norse, Linda King, and Jon and Gypsy Lou Webb, from Loudon Press. Other poets like Steve Richmond and Neeli Cherkovski also found themselves in disfavor with Hank, only to later be brought back into his good graces.

The fact remains however, that Hank was hurt by what I wrote. I believe in his heart he felt I had betrayed him. He responded by writing a poem titled "Poem for the Poet up North", which was published in *Impulse*, a small Southern California literary magazine. The gist of the poem was that he had once shared a few drinks with me (before he became successful), and because he later gained literary fame that this somehow "gnawed" away at me. He couldn't have been more wrong. I responded with a poem of my own ("Poem For the Poet Down South"), which *Impulse* magazine also published. As far as I'm aware, this ended the feud between us, and the attacks went no further. Hank went about his life doing what he did best, writing his poetry and prose, while I went about my life as an Equal Opportunity Specialist for the Department of Education, Office for Civil Rights.

My duties were to investigate discrimination claims against minorities, women and the disabled, while writing my own poetry as time permitted.

Now here I found myself sitting alone in my small apartment with Hank on my mind. I walked over to the bookcase and removed the special Charles Bukowski issue I had published in 1974, and began thumbing through it, which brought back fond memories of those early years. I recalled when friends and fellow writers raved about Hank's poetry, that I would urge them to read his prose. I find his prose to be fast, concise, gripping, and frequently laced with humor. In my opinion, his prose is more concise and disciplined than his poetry, which at times has a tendency to ramble on, and too often reflects forced endings. This does not diminish the fact that many of his poems are as powerful as any poem I have read.

Taking a break and switching from coffee to beer, I

remembered Hank's "I Am With The Roots Of Flowers," which appeared in issue One of *The Outsider* magazine. I believe the year was 1961. This may have been the first time I realized his raw power as a poet and writer.

As I continued to read Hank's work that day, I was reminded I had informed him F. Scott Fitzgerald and Ernest Hemingway had influenced me. Hank confided in me that he found Fitzgerald's work too "polished," but acknowledged being influenced by the writings of Hemingway, no doubt perhaps also influenced by his manly ways and life style.

The honesty of Hank's work hooked me from the very beginning. If his work was not always beautiful, it was certainly honest and moving. The same can be said for his letters. Letter writing has become a lost art (especially since e-mail), but Hank's letters are collector items, fetching top dollar on the open market. They are frequently laced with brilliance. To put it simply, Hank was always a good read.

I became an avid fan of his after reading his first novel, *Post Office*. I worked at the San Francisco Rincon Annex post office for five years, from 1959 until 1964, and Hank's vivid accounts of his eleven years as a postal clerk hit home with me like a brick.

Hank found it necessary to drink and get drunk in order to survive those years, much the same as I had, but what most impressed me about the book was his ability to laugh at those painful days, and in a wild and beautiful way.

I admire the fact that, in 1970 at the age of forty-nine, he took the big gamble and quit the post office to devote full time to his writing. It would be the turning point in his life. He took the big gamble and won. No more punching time clocks. No more having to deal with career bosses whose only purpose in life seemed to be making workers miserable.

Shutting out all thoughts of the post office, I cut out Hank's obituary and tossed the newspaper aside. I walked into the kitchen and returned to the living room with a bottle of brandy. I settled back into my easy chair and began reading the over eighty letters he wrote me during the seventies and eighties. As I did so, I cursed myself for not keeping carbon copies of the letters I had written him over those same years.

As I continued to drink, my mind wandered back to the first issue of Second *Coming,* which I had sent him in the hope he would send me some poems I might be able to use in the second issue of the magazine.

Second Coming was dedicated to publishing all schools of poetry, but it was Hank who defined what I was trying to accomplish as an editor and publisher of a literary magazine that *Library Journal* described as one of the best small press magazines of its day. The magazine, which later expanded to include the publishing of books, would survive for seventeen years. How good was the magazine?

The late Richard Morris, author and long time director of the now defunct Committee of Small Magazine Editors and Publishers (COSMEP) said: "The two most significant influences on contemporary West Coast writing have been the Beats and Charles Bukowski.

Both of them were reflected in the writing published in *Second Coming* as it became the most important San Francisco literary magazine of its era."

High praise indeed, but Hank himself was quoted as listing *Second Coming, New York* Quarterly and the *Wormwood Review* as three of the best literary magazines for serious writers interested in submitting their work. I would add John Bennett's *Vagabond* to the list.

When I finished reading the last of his letters to me, I made a decision to write a book about my experiences with Hank and his importance to *Second Coming.* This was a time in history when small presses were producing some of the best poetry being written (some of the worst too), and I consider his letters to be historically important to small press history. Hank's publisher (during his life), John Martin, would confirm this in a letter he wrote me after I mailed him a rough draft of my book, *The Holy Grail: Charles Bukowski And The Second Coming Revolution.*

"Thanks for sending this for me to read. The quotes are fine. No problems at all. It's a straightforward piece of writing and is valuable for what it says about Bukowski and the problems of small press publishing back in the seventies and eighties."

The book would first be published by Beat Scene in England, and later republished (in an expanded edition) by Len Fulton's Dust Books. It was not just another book about Hank, but about his relationship with me and *Second Coming,* and expanded beyond this to document the trials of the small presses in the seventies and eighties, while at the same time paying tribute to the poets and writers who made *Second Coming* the success it was.

During our friendship I had extensive talks with Hank on the role the critic plays in the small press. Hank believed in the end the only valid criticism is a better piece of work.

On the telephone and in person we both questioned the motives of small press critics, having too often found ourselves in the company of critics at parties and at poetry readings. We were dismayed at the army of vultures who preferred to review the poet and his life style, rather than the work itself. We agreed if a writer worked long enough and was lucky enough to get published and gain a bit of fame that in the end he would be unlucky enough to draw the attention of the critics.

The late Charles McCabe, a columnist for the *San Francisco Chronicle,* referred to these individuals as "time gobblers," people who would stop at nothing to put the knife in you. Like McCabe, Hank believed if these critics couldn't attack your work, they would attack your personal life, and having nothing to do in their own lives they would fill their time by devouring yours.

At parties, if you looked close enough, you'd notice they didn't drink, but sipped; they didn't eat food, they nibbled at it; they didn't make love, they violated.

McCabe said, "Their basic assumption seems to be that because you have become a public figure, no matter how small, that they have somehow earned the right to own a piece of you."

"At parties or at receptions they try to corner you, boring you with stories of their own dull lives, and demanding to know more about yours."

McCabe felt the worst part was their intent to record your every thought and action, so they might later play it back to the world, "taking delight in writing that age had destroyed your ability to write, and that you were old and burned out."

Hank, like McCabe, believed there was only one way to deal with this kind of critic, short of maiming or killing him, and this was to treat him with brutality. I argued this approach would only cheapen you and add another enemy to a growing list.

Hank argued that at least it would rid you of the critic, whom McCabe had described as being, "the most odious specimen on earth. A thief who would steal your belongings is nothing compared to the critic who would steal your soul with no remorse."

Hank felt it was a mistake to show these people the slightest bit of kindness, believing they would mistake any kindness for weakness, and go for the jugular vein. As it turned out, Hank didn't have much reason to fear the critics. The small presses lavished praise on him, while the academic community simply ignored him.

As I said earlier I only met him in person a few times. The main thrust of our relationship was through personal correspondence and telephone conversations. I made an early decision to limit any personal contact with him, knowing how much he valued his privacy. I never forced myself on him, realizing he didn't like the endless crowd of poets who frequently knocked on his door, robbing him of valuable time he felt could better be spent on his writing.

However, the few times I met him were memorable ones, like the poetry reading in the seventies (the dates have faded over the years) sponsored by City Lights Publishing House, which was held at the Telegraph Hill Neighborhood Association Hall. There was a large turnout that night. Perhaps three hundred or more people had come to hear their hero read.

I can still picture the polished wooden floor and the noisy and anxious crowd waiting on his arrival. The majority of the audience was younger in age, with maybe a third or more of the crowd made up of older literary figures, many of who were stoned on alcohol or drugs.

What I recall most about the evening was the stage setting. It was furnished with a simple chair, a folding table, a microphone, and a refrigerator filled with cold beer.

I later learned the refrigerator with beer was Hank's asking price for doing the reading that evening.

I watched him milk the crowd for all it was worth before he appeared from back stage to a cheering crowd. Once on stage, he wasted no time in opening the refrigerator door and popping open a can of beer to the sound of wild cheers. I watched him survey the crowd for several seconds before tilting back his head and drinking half the contents from the beer can. Again this simple act was met with rousing cheers. I continued to watch as he raised his hand to quiet the crowd, a tactic that failed to work.

Hank slowly took his place at the table. He began the reading with a poem filled with the kind of language the audience had come to hear. He read the kind of poems his army of fans had come to identify him with, and finished the last poem to loud applause as he crushed the empty beer can in one of his ham hock hands and tossed it to the side of the stage.

I recall thinking that no one could open a can of beer like Hank did.

During the reading, I would estimate he consumed as many as twelve cans of beer. If there was anything else in the refrigerator, other than beer, I couldn't make it out. In retrospect, the event reminded me of the first Monterey Jazz Festival I had attended as a young man. At the time, I was in awe of the musicians, just as the crowd that night was hypnotized by Hank.

He appeared to be enjoying the attention he was receiving, but this may have partly been attributed to his drinking. I say this only because he (despite his reputation) was a shy man in those early days when it came to giving public readings. It was the alcohol, and the alcohol alone, that provided him with the bravado he displayed on stage.

There was a lot of shit and fuck poems, and some cute and clever ones, and after each poem, he grinned at the audience, at times resembling a leprechaun. It was a night that left the North Beach crowd buzzing long after he left the stage on his way to a party at the home of the poet Lawrence Ferlinghetti.

Ferlinghetti's apartment was located on upper Grant Avenue, directly over the old City Lights Publishing House. Hank and Linda King, who was his lover at the time, would later get into a violent argument. The argument became physical, with Hank being pushed or falling down a flight of stairs, depending on whether you believe Hank or Linda King's version of what happened. Either way, his face was badly scratched.

During the confrontation, a window was broken, and the story goes that Lawrence was pissed at both Hank and Linda, but any ill feelings quickly passed.

I wasn't at the party when the fight broke out, so I have to rely on what Linda King told Harold Norse in a letter Norse later published in his highly acclaimed literary journal *Bastard Angel*. To quote from Linda King's letter:

"I think I would kill him (Bukowski) if he wasn't so good in bed. I didn't claw his face . . he hit somewhere when he fell . .I was defending my innocent self . .I did do the biting."

Whatever the truth may be, Hank and Linda King had

a long and quarreling relationship. Linda said Hank's sensitivities were too raw, and he would try to dull them with alcohol. She told Norse their two tempers would explode like shooting geysers, and they would roar down another emotional roller coaster with one more fight and one more split-up.

But the separations never lasted long. From Linda King's letter:

"After several hundred dollars in telephone calls and a new woman for Bukowski and one night stands for me, we would go back to being lovers."

"It was the raw magic of sex that kept us together as long as it did. It's not because he's a great poet. He is, I know that. It's all that magic between the sheets, in the afternoon, in the morning, at midnight, the real poetry."

As for Hank, he said it best in a letter he wrote to the poet Jack Micheline.

"I'm really in love with this sculptress, this Linda King, man, and she writes poetry too.

"When we split, I just about go crazy. Fucking real deep down pain-agony, babe; all the coals burning, all the knifes going in, more horrible than any cancer death, that feeling, first feeling like that I've had since the death of Jane. Most women can't get to me, but this one does. Real mountain-tall magic, and most splits are my fault. I go crazy, walk out on her .and then she leaves town or I can't find her. It's all too much, but I'm glad it's here. It wasn't meant to last, but it was a wild memorable trip."

The most memorable of the times I spent with Hank was during an unexpected visit he paid me in the seventies. He wanted to visit North Beach, but didn't want to drink at the bars, afraid he would run into any number of San Francisco poets he wanted to avoid.

Hank seemed fascinated with North Beach, as I took him on a tour of the long gone beat bars and hangouts that had once flourished: the Coffee Gallery (now The Lost and Found Bar), The Co-Existence Bagel Shop, Mike's Pool Hall, The Place, and the San Gottardo Hotel and Bar run by an elderly French couple.

I pointed out the few bars still remaining, Vesuvio's: Gino and Carlo's, Spec's, and The Saloon. As we walked up Grant Avenue, we occasionally ran into poets and North Beach regulars whom I had known since the fifties and sixties. We found Paddy O'Sullivan talking to the bartender at the Camel's Bar, on the corner of Grant and Green, and stopped in to chat with him. Paddy was one of the more colorful characters of the Beat era, a minor poet who supported himself by hawking a pocket-sized book of his poems titled *Weep Not My Child*.

You could find Paddy almost any night of the week standing on the corner dressed in a purple cape, plumed hat, and high boots, with long shoulder-length hair. He was a modern-day cavalier who greeted female tourists with a courteous bow and a kiss on the hand. Rumor has it Paddy was nothing more than a self-created myth, who followed Greenwich Village poet Maxwell Bodenheim around and stole his poems when Bodenheim died.

If you asked Paddy about this, he would respond with a sly smile. He was a legend in North Beach. He would later lose his arm to a pet cheetah, but never lost his charm. When Paddy went to the men's room, Hank said it was people like him who gave poetry a bad name. Maybe so, I thought, but I will always remember the night at the Camel's bar, when I was stone drunk, and how Paddy had saved me from a beating at the hands of a local bully.

Paddy was very protective of the people he liked, and had more strength in his one arm than some people have with both. He quickly subdued the bully in a headlock and threw him out into the street. When I told Hank this story, he said, "Well, maybe he can't write poetry, and maybe it's all a game, but he sounds like the kind of a guy I'd like to have watching my back."

I would later write a poem dedicated to him.

PADDY O'SULLIVAN

Paddy O'Sullivan

Home again wearing

The scars of the past

Like an engraved bracelet

Passed on from one lover

To the next

Paddy O'Sullivan walking

The streets of North Beach

In search of old visions

Now only memories

In the nightmare of reality

Paddy O'Sullivan swapping tales

With obscene priests

Hung over with failure

Paddy O'Sullivan of Kerouac tales

And Cassady adventures

Walking Washington Square

The bulldozer death

Lurking everywhere

Paddy O'Sullivan

Does your typewriter still

Talk to you

In the early hours of dawn

Paddy O'Sullivan

Alone in San Francisco

Waiting on that lady poet

Who will forgive you

In the morning

For forgetting her name

In the hour of dawn

When our needs are soothed

With the power

Of the written word

That stirs moves inside us

Like a runaway train

Like the haunting breath

Of a hound dog closing in

For the kill

Paddy O'Sullivan where

Have all the poets gone

Walking straight jackets

Trapped by time

Paddy O'Sullivan

The sun is not

As you see it now

Everything changes

And yet remains the same

The streets are no more

Or less intense

The lines on your face

Are the lines on my face

As we move back

Into the body

Into the inner self

Measured by the amnesia

Of yesterday

Paddy O'Sullivan

This town coughs up

Its dead most rudely

The raw nerve of time

Returning to haunt me

Oblivious to the thirst

Lying still at the edge

Of the river

The blueprint of life

Etched in the dark deep

Shadows of the soul

Hank and I left the bar before Paddy returned from the men's room. We walked down the street to Gino and Carlo's Bar owned by two Italian brothers, Aldino and Dinado. We stopped outside to talk with Carl Eisenger, a sad figure of a man. Carl was a poet, but hadn't written in years, after his life's work was destroyed in a hotel room fire. He hadn't kept carbon copies of his poems, and his life had literally gone up in flames.

Hank and I entered Gino and Carlo's bar, where we found Cheap Charlie lying on the floor in a drunken stupor. Cheap Charlie had gotten his name because of his mooching free drinks at North Beach bars. Hank and I looked at Aldino, who was leaning over the body of Cheap Charlie and pouring whiskey through a funnel down Cheap Charlie's throat as the patrons cheered him on.

"Are all the poets in this area crazy?" Hank asked.

"Not all of them," I said.

We left the bar and headed down Grant Avenue, stopping in front of the 1232 Club, also known as the Saloon. Shoeshine Divine was standing outside, clutching his custom made shoeshine box.

Shoeshine was another colorful North Beach figure. who later confided that he was wanted by the FBI for draft evasion, which may or may not have been the truth

Jerry Kamstra, author of The Frisco Kid, said in his book that what made Shoeshine different from most people who shine shoes for a living is that he didn't sit on a stool, but instead squatted in front of his customers, bouncing up and down like a yo-yo. I exchanged a few barbs with Shoeshine, whom Hank later said had a wild look in his eyes. The kind of look that Hank said he had seen on the faces of men he had gotten drunk with during his stone drunk days.

As Shoeshine walked away, Bob Seider happened to pass by, asking for some spare change. Hank reached into his pocket and handed Seider some loose coins. Seider thanked Hank and hurried off in the direction of the old

Coffee Gallery. Hank said he didn't normally make it a habit to give handouts to street bums, but there was something in Seider's eyes that set him apart from the others. I told him Seider had been one of the few white jazz musicians who had frequented the North Beach jazz joints in the old Beat days. He had played at all the small jazz clubs, at the beach, charming the regulars with his smile and friendly manner. If you weren't lucky enough to catch him playing his sax at the North Beach clubs, you could watch him perform free on the street, near Washington Square Park, where he liked to hang out. Then one day he pawned his sax and quit playing forever.

We walked to the Cafe Trieste, where Hank stopped and peered in at a small group of men and women sitting at the intimately spaced tables. Without warning, he said in a loud voice:

"Look at all these people waiting for something to happen, only it never will."

He hurried away without waiting for a response, leaving me behind to overhear a skinny woman with glasses make an insensitive remark. "God, did you see all that acne? What a drinker's nose. He'll be dead before you know it."

The remark was met with a smattering of laughter, as the young woman continued drinking her espresso. She was dead wrong! Hank's scars weren't from acne, but childhood boils, and he would live a relatively full life for a man who abused his body as much as he did.

Hank was under the impression the Beat movement began with Kerouac, Ginsberg, Cassady and the long list of Beats that the media helped make famous. There are others who would disagree.

John Pyros, a writer friend, argues that the Beat movement could be said to have evolved on August 6, 1945, when the first atomic bomb was dropped on Hiroshima, and to have ended in 1967 with the Human Be-in in San Francisco during the last days of the Hippie generation.

Perhaps the single most important thing Kerouac, Ginsberg and Cassady did was to make other rebellious young people throughout the land aware that there were others out there who felt the same way they did.

Diane di Prima is quoted as saying after she read Howl:

"I sensed he (Ginsberg) was only , could only be the vanguard of a much larger thing. All the people, who like me, had hidden and skulked. All these people would now step forward and say their piece. Not many would hear them, but they would, finally, hear each other. I was about to meet my brothers."

John Pyros, perhaps put it best:

"To state that Kerouac and Ginsberg, et al began the Beat movement is like saying that Rosa Parks started the Civil Rights Movement . . . In fact, the land was fertile and awaited only the seed, only the spark to be kindled."

While Hank seemed curious about the neighborhood the Beats frequented, he did not particularly seem interested in learning the history of the Beat movement. I tried to get him to have a beer with me at the Vesuvio bar, located adjacent to City Lights Bookstore, which had been a favorite hangout of the Beats, but he declined.

As we continued our walk through North Beach, I clued him in on the history of City Lights Bookstore, which was founded in the fifties by Peter Martin (who later sold his interest) and Lawrence Ferlinghetti.

In the beginning, the bookstore was mostly visited by Italian anarchists, people Martin was familiar with, being the son of an Italian Anarchist, Carlo Tresca, assassinated in 1943. Ferlinghetti too associated with the anarchist writers, many of who were friends or acquaintances of Kenneth Rexroth, referred to by many as the father of the Beats. City Lights began as the first all-paperback bookstore in the U.S. Even in those days cloth copies of books were relatively expensive and out of the reach of many working-class people. Martin suggested naming the store City Lights, taking the name from a Charlie Chaplin film.

City Lights sprang into prominence on March 25, 1957, when the San Francisco District Attorney's office decided to take City Lights and its owners to court after Allen Ginsberg's *Howl and Other Poems* (printed in England) was seized by the U.S. Customs in San Francisco, whose criminal division decided the book was obscene. The case never went to court after the U.S. district attorney refused to prosecute, forcing Federal Customs officials to release the books.

The San Francisco police, however, refused to ignore the matter. Ferlinghetti and Shig Muro (who at the time managed City Lights) were arrested and charged with selling obscene literature.

The American Civil Liberties Union stepped in and furnished free legal representation, providing the famed attorney Jake Ehrich to defend them. Prominent writers and critics testified in court on behalf of City Lights, and Judge Clayton Horn set the legal precedent that if a book has the slightest redeeming social importance, it is protected under the First and Fourteenth Amendment of the U.S. and the California constitutions and therefore cannot be declared obscene. This legal precedent allowed D.H. Lawrence's *Lady Chatterley's Lover* and Henry Miller's *Tropic of Cancer* (long banned in the U.S.) to be published by Grove Press.

The San Francisco police had unwittingly helped put City Lights and Lawrence Ferlinghetti on the map. Not learning their lesson, the police returned in the sixties, to focus their attention on *Zap Comics* and Lenore Kandal's *Love Poems,* which only served to sell out both publications

Hank wanted to grab a bite to eat before leaving the beach, and I suggested Chinatown, which would be free of the poets Hank wanted to avoid.

I decided to take him to Sam Woo's, a three-story

restaurant, where you had to walk through the kitchen in order to make your way to the upstairs dining room. The food was brought up to you on a dumb waiter.

The restaurant was one of the most popular eating places in the city, after the noted newspaper columnist, Herb Caen wrote up the waiter, Edsel Ford, a colorful person who ruled over the restaurant. As we walked through the kitchen, filled with non-English speaking Chinese cooks with meat cleavers in their hands, Hank said, "I hope the hell you know what you're doing."

"Don't worry," I said, leading him upstairs to the dining area, where Edsel Ford, the headwaiter, greeted us. Edsel was part entertainer, part waiter, and part mad man. He told the patrons where to sit, and what to order, and if you didn't like it, you were free to leave. The food was only ordinary, but the restaurant was always filled to capacity.

Edsel nodded to me in recognition as Hank walked at my side. Suddenly Edsel turned and shouted at Hank, "Single file. Single file. You stupid?" Hank was caught off guard, at first growing angry, and then smiling, sensing it was all part of an act.

Edsel led us to a booth at the back of the restaurant and thrust a menu in our hands. I don't remember what Hank ordered, except he wanted a side bowl of steamed rice, and that Edsel flashed him a menacing look.

"No white rice. No white rice," Edsel bellowed.

"Who ever heard of a Chinese restaurant that doesn't serve rice?" Hank loudly bellowed. He finally settled on a plate of noodles, which were the best noodles in Chinatown.

After lunch, I slipped Edsel a fiver and asked him to "spike" the tea. He smiled and returned with an 86% proof laced pot of tea. Hank poured himself a drink and said, "I think I could grow to like that guy."

We spent a considerable amount of time talking about Hank's favorite subject, women. I can't remember much of the conversation, but when I talked about losing a woman that I still loved to another man, Hank grew serious.

"You have no idea what it's like really like to lose a woman. When Jane died, I knew I would never again be the same. It's too painful to put down in prose. I try to write it down on paper, but it never comes out right. I never want to bury another woman again."

Hank talked about fame. He said becoming famous was not important to him, but he would like to someday own a place of his own, even if it was only a shack. He talked about his fear of dying alone, and said he hoped when his time came they would discover his body early and not find him week's later bloated and covered with flies.

Hank felt it was durability that counted and boasted he had outlived many of the editors who had rejected his work early on in the game. We talked about the small presses.

Hank spoke highly of the old *Wormwood Review* and *Nola Express,* saying the latter had paid him a small sum of money for his prose pieces that had appeared in the small publication, and that this had helped him in his later decision to quit his job with the post office.

We talked about drugs and whether they were good for you or not. My experience with drugs was limited to grass, uppers and downers, and single experiences with peyote and LSD. Hank admitted to using drugs, but was negative about using cocaine, which he felt was destructive. He said the only drug he was addicted to was alcohol, but found that unlike other drugs, it didn't interfere with his writing.

I told him about my first night at North beach, after I had returned home from Panama (1958) after completing my military obligation. The first bar I drank at was a beer and wine bar called the Coffee Gallery. I was astonished at the dress of the people I saw at the bar. The women were basically dressed in black. The men wore sandals, berets, and sunglasses. It was if they were sending out a signal they were not "square", that they were not part of the success-orientated general population.

Later, I wandered down to the Anxious Asp, which was a Beat hangout, and was again amazed by the mingling of black men with white women. Despite San Francisco's liberal reputation, this was not something that was openly practiced in public.

From the Anxious Asp, I made my way down the street to the San Gottardo Hotel and bar. The bar was packed that night, but I managed to make my way past the crowd. I bellied-up to the bar and ordered a beer.

Before I could taste my first drink, I felt someone from behind, tugging at my shirt. I turned around and saw a woman in her thirties smiling at me.

"You want to fuck?" She asked.

Before I could respond, I found myself being taken by the hand and led upstairs to one of the rented hotel rooms. In short order, we were naked and making love. I was only twenty-two and spent the next few hours locked in animal passion. Later we went downstairs for a nightcap and learned of a party going on at a warehouse, in the produce district.

At the party, we went our separate ways. The room was thick with smoke, making it uncomfortable for me. I wandered into the kitchen and poured myself a drink from one of several jugs of wine sitting on the kitchen table.

Returning to the living room, I saw a group of men and women gathered in a circle, sharing a joint. In the far corner of the room, a young black dude was dry-humping a fat Japanese woman, whose blouse was open, exposing her ample breasts. I walked closer to the black male and his Japanese woman friend. They soon discarded their clothes and began making love with no thought of the small crowd that had gathered around to watch them. Finally the black dude climbed off the woman and moved down the hall, where he disappeared into an adjacent room.

I poured myself another drink and went into the room. I was startled to find the black dude and a well-built white man naked and groping each other. I felt like an uninvited voyeur and returned to the main room, where I saw the Japanese woman sleeping on the floor.

Shortly afterwards, I fell asleep. When I woke up the next morning, the sun was rising, and I could hear the nine-to-five people on their way to work. The Japanese woman was still asleep on the floor. I hadn't even read Jack Kerouac's *On The Road,* and here I was living it.

Hank brought up the earlier incident at the Cafe Trieste. He said Los Angeles had its fair share of pretentious coffee houses, but he had made it a point to stay away from them. He described coffee houses as haunts for talent-less poets and pseudo-intellectuals, whom he described as "soft boiled egg and parsley eaters."

The conversation shifted to the brawls Hank had gotten into as a teenager, when Hank said he had been forced to defend himself because of his pock-faced looks.

Later Hank lived in the slum streets of Los Angeles where survival meant being able to take care of one's self.

"Not unlike Hell's Kitchen in Chicago," Hank said.

In *Poetry Now*, Bukowski is quoted as saying:

"The trouble is I liked it. I liked the impact of knuckles against teeth, of feeling the terrific lightning that breaks in your brain when somebody lands a clean one and you have to try to shake loose and come back and nail him before he finishes you off."

We finished the spiked tea and left the restaurant in good spirits, walking up to Grant Avenue where I had parked my car and drove him to the motel he was staying at. We shook hands and promised to stay in touch.

The next time I saw him was at a poetry reading in San Francisco, where he read to a sold out audience. I was given a free back stage pass, but paid the $3 ticket fee, since I believe in supporting poets. I stood back stage and watched the old man play the crowd for all it was worth. I later would write a poem titled, "I Paid $3 to see Bukowski Read And Then Went Back Stage And Got In Free."

The poem was published in the *New York Quarterly*, which caused Hank to write and tell me he liked "the pure honesty" of the poem. The poem was a virtual newspaper-like accounting of the reading Hank gave that evening and the party that followed the reading. The kind of poem Hank himself might write.

The reading resembled a circus. Hank repeated his beer drinking performance of old, spending much of the time engaged in verbal jousting with a small group of radical female feminists who had come to the reading to taunt him. The women never stood a chance, and the hostile crowd quickly booed them into silence even though Hank defended them to the audience.

Jack Micheline, a long-time friend of Hank, was present in the audience and tried to get Hank to let him read a poem. Hank would have none of it. It was his show and he wasn't about to share it with anyone. Jack had to settle for vomiting on the shoe of a minor local poet. That was the kind of night it was.

At the end of the reading, Hank bowed and thanked the audience, while a young man in the back of the hall began shouting, "More, More."

Hank flashed the young man an impish smile.

"How much did you pay to get into the reading?" he asked. The kid took the bait. "$3.00," he said. "And you're a $3 audience," Hank shot back, much to the delight of the crowd.

Hank exited the building by means of the back stage, where we warmly embraced each other, much to the envious looks of several San Francisco poets who had come to hear him read with the hope they might gain a sense of importance by being seen with him. Hank asked me to ride with him in a van to a party that was being held in his honor, but I politely declined.

I had parked my car a short distance from the reading and drove to the party alone. When I arrived at the party, it was wall-to-wall bodies and the usual crowd. There were the poets who were intensely jealous of the old man, mixed in with the poets who were seeking instant fame, even though their limited talent made this next to impossible. And the young women were there too, the women who had made it once too often, in bedrooms, in hallways, in alleyways, and in bathrooms, with pushed-up skirts and knees scarred from one too many head jobs. And the old enemies were there too.

I watched John Bryan edge his way close to Hank, whispering in a low voice, "You better watch it, my wife is here with a knife." John had told me earlier that Hank had tried to put the make on his wife (Joanie) at a time when he and Hank were still friends. I don't know if this is true or not. Hank would neither confirm nor deny it.

Hank shrugged off Bryan's remark and said, "Can't you forget, that was in the old days?" But Bryan couldn't forget, because Hank had made it and Bryan hadn't.

There were enough poets in the room to make up a professional football team. There were poets from San Francisco and poets from Berkeley, even one poet from New York, taking down notes on everything Hank said. It was a carnival-like atmosphere.

I found my attention drawn to three women in the middle of the room. One of the women was in the company of a male slave, who was naked from the waist up and wearing a dog collar around his neck.

I was amused to see the slave had a leather leash attached to the dog collar, which his mistress held securely in one hand. The young man stood at near attention, his eyes staring down at the wooden floor. None of the women spoke to or looked at him. No one at the party paid them the slightest attention, but that's the way it is in San- Francisco, where people have become accustomed to the bizarre.

I watched Hank surrounded by men and women alike. It was as if he was a rock star, and everyone wanted to reach out and touch him. The movie *Jesus Christ Super Star* comes to mind, and I thought I could see a pained look on his face.

It wasn't a night for serious conversation, and it wasn't long before he drank himself into a semi-coma, perhaps the only way to keep sane among the crowd of people who had gathered around him like hungry cannibals, feasting on his every word.

After consuming a few beers, I had to fight my way to the bathroom, only to find the room occupied in an unusual manner. The leather-clad mistress and her male slave were in the bathtub. The slave was naked and lying on his back. The woman was crouched on the upper part of the bathtub, straddling him in an awkward position, holding her skirt up, and forcing her slave to endure the indignity of a golden shower. I pretended not to look as I embarrassingly relieved myself.

When I was through taking care of business, I went into the kitchen to get myself a beer. Micheline was standing next to the refrigerator, surrounded by a group of admirers. Next to Hank, Micheline was second in demand; a silver-haired New York Bronx poet whom the poetry crowd in San Francisco adopted as one of there own.

He was talking to a young woman who was visiting from Australia, telling her tales of the old Beat days. When Jack spotted me, he motioned for me to come over and join him. I let him introduce me to the young woman, and then watched him leave the room to discuss business with Hank.

I was surprised when the young woman unbuttoned lher blouse, revealing two magnificent breasts, with silver dollar nipples. She invited me to touch them, telling me they were for real. Within minutes we were kissing, and I felt her hand at my crotch, when she suddenly broke free and told me she was on antibiotics.

She asked me for my telephone number and said she would give me a call when she was well. I tucked it into my shirt pocket and watched her leave the kitchen to talk to a young poet who was without success trying to get Hank's attention.

In no time at all, I had a good buzz on. I returned to the bathroom, where I found Hank sitting on the commode, a young woman on her knees, giving him a blowjob. His eyes were closed, but there was definitely a smile on his face. He would later write me and say he didn't remember getting a blowjob, but he hoped it had been a good one.

Hank gave one last reading in San Francisco, which was organized by Kathleen Fraser, who at the time was the Director of the San Francisco State University Poetry Center. For reasons that still elude me, Fraser scheduled William Stafford, a respected academic poet, to read on the same bill with Hank. Hanks dislike for academic poets was well known and I smelled disaster in the air.

On the night of the reading, I met him outside the Veteran's Auditorium, a strange place for a poetry reading. Hank was scheduled to read after Stafford and told me he didn't want to listen to Stafford read, so I accompanied him across the street to a small bar called The Jury Room. We sat at a table across from the jukebox and ordered a round of screwdrivers. During the second round of drinks, we discussed the poetry scene in San Francisco, focusing on several San Francisco poets Hank disliked. He seemed relieved when he learned I too held these same poets in low esteem. I remember he seemed nervous and tense, and at times the conversation seemed forced.

Hank had the keys to a friend's van, which was parked in an alley not far from the Veteran's Auditorium. After a few drinks, we left the bar, and walked to the van where Hank had stashed away a pint of vodka in the back seat.

Hank sat in the back of the van while I sat in the front seat. I watched him reach under the back seat and remove a pint bottle of vodka, downing half the bottle in less than thirty seconds. I was surprised when he refused to share the bottle with me.

He leaned toward me and said, "A. D., I need every drop to see me through the reading. If it weren't for the money, I wouldn't give these damn things. I'm like a beggar singing for his supper."

While we sat in the van, we discussed the things we had in common. We had both been arrested for driving under the influence of alcohol, and both of us had spent time in the drunk tank, twice for me and several times for Hank.

We both had been forced to attend traffic school and had our driver's license suspended. And both of us disliked giving poetry readings. Hank felt San Francisco poets were so eager for attention they begged like seals to read at every opportunity, even at open "mic" readings. He said he guessed this was all right for poets who were just starting out, but that poetry was a profession, and too many poets prostituted it.

"Can you imagine a carpenter coming over to your home and working on your house for free?" Hank asked. He couldn't understand why a poet would get up on stage and bare his soul unless he was paid for it.

I recall feeling overwhelmed by him. There was something awesome about him. His shoulders were stooped over from the years. His hair was starting to thin; his face was a road map of scarred pock marks, but his smile and wit soon put me at ease.

We went on to discuss other things we shared in common. Hank had gone to Los Angeles City College, while I had attended City College of San Francisco. We both had unhappy childhoods, but unlike Hank, my father had never laid a hand on me. and we both had a large appetite when it came to women. We discussed the women we had scored with and the ones who had scorned us.

We discussed Hank's work that had earlier appeared in the *Outsider* magazine and the *Los Angeles Free Press*. I told him how impressed I had been on reading his "Notes Of A Dirty Old Man." He thanked me, but said he didn't want to talk about the column, nevertheless expressing gratitude he had been paid a small sum of money for his efforts.

I watched him work his way down to the bottom of the vodka bottle. He complained another reason he hated giving poetry readings was the organizers always expected him to attend a party afterwards. Hank said he didn't know why he attended the parties because they were almost always boring. Remembering the party Ferlinghetti had hosted and the party I had witnessed the male slave being urinated on, I found this hard to believe.

Letting out a loud sigh, Hank finished the last of the vodka, tossing the bottle on the floor of the van. Hank said, "It's time to pay the piper," but we didn't get ten feet outside the vehicle before he turned and vomited on the side of the van. I asked him if he was okay. He told me not to worry, that it was normal for him to vomit before a reading. He said, "It helps steady the nerves," but I wasn't sure if he was serious or not.

Hank straightened himself up and looked perfectly sober as we made our way to the Veteran's Auditorium. As we entered the building, I suggested we sit in the back of the auditorium, so we would not disturb William Stafford's reading, but Hank insisted on taking seats closer to the front stage.

When the crowd caught sight of Hank walking down the aisle, they began chanting: "BUK. BUK. BUK."

It was as if the heavyweight champion of the world was entering the ring to do battle.

Stafford paused momentarily before continuing on with his reading. I felt badly for Stafford. It wasn't that I liked his poetry, which was far too academic for my taste, but I felt he deserved more respect from Hank; on the other hand Hank felt no remorse at all. If anything, he seemed to enjoy the attention he was receiving from the boisterous crowd.

We took seats near the front of the stage as Stafford finished his reading and exited the building. I watched Hank push his way past the people in our row and lumber slowly on to the stage.

He stood to one side as the Master of Ceremonies introduced him to thunderous applause. Flash bulbs were popping everywhere, and the heavy emotion of the audience seemed heartfelt. Hank played the audience like the master he was, smiling at the right times, tossing in jives and raw language for shock value, and reading for about forty-five minutes.

As usual, he gave a dynamite reading. When he finished his reading, he was greeted with chants of: "MORE, MORE. MORE." Hank read one last poem, before exiting the stage, eager for another drink.

After the reading, I accompanied him back across the street, where we resumed our earlier drinking. In between drinks, we discussed the need for a writer to be alone.

Hank was of the opinion that what it came down to in the end was the writer alone in his home with his typewriter, and that everything else was a distraction. He described writer workshops as lonely heart clubs for writers who would never amount to anything.

"Name me one major writer who has come out of a writer's workshop?" Hank asked me?

John Corrington is quoted as saying: "A Bukowski poem is like the spoken voice nailed to paper." It's hard to argue with this viewpoint. How do you teach something like this at a writer's workshop? The truth is Hank wrote poetry in a language the average person could understand and identify with, thus his appeal to the ordinary masses.

Hank quickly finished his drink, and asked me if I could drive him to the airport. As it turned out, I didn't need to drive him there. A young man who claimed to be a documentary filmmaker convinced Hank to stay the night at his place, supposedly to work out the details on the proposed documentary.

I got up from the table and shook hands with Hank, leaving him with the filmmaker, as I headed outside to my car and headed home.

There would be one final meeting with Hank, which took place in Los Angeles at the home of Linda King. Hank invited me to visit with him and Linda, and agreed to sign a small number of copies of the special Charles Bukowski *Second Coming* issue.

I arrived early in Los Angeles, stopping off at several bars to pass the time away. When I arrived at Linda King's home it was just beginning to turn dark.

I was in the company of a writer acquaintance who had pleaded with me to take him to meet Buk. Hank greeted RB and me at the front door. I immediately sensed Hank did not like RB. He had seen something about him that had escaped me.

Hank and Linda were in the company of a young male, barely out of his teens. The kid sat alone, in an armchair, in the far corner of the room throughout my entire visit, and I don't recall his saying a single word.

Hank said he had no idea who the kid was. The young man had shown up at their doorstep early that morning wanting to meet Hank. Linda and Hank had agreed to let him sleep the night on the couch, but Hank insisted the kid would be shown the door the first thing in the morning.

Throughout the evening, one of them would excuse themselves to go into the kitchen and return with a fresh round of drinks. I found my own writing dissected at great length, and at times felt uncomfortable. I didn't like being so closely scrutinized, and had I been sober, I'm sure I would have gotten up and left. I guess I passed the test, for as the evening wore on, things began to mellow out, and the atmosphere became more relaxed and friendly.

And during the entire visit, the kid in the corner never said a word, hardly looking our way.

We spent a considerable amount of time discussing Jack Micheline and his place in literature. I argued Jack's work had been unfairly ignored, and that he was equally as good or better than many of the Beat poets who had gained a measure of fame. On this count, Hank and I agreed.

It became obvious to me that Hank liked Jack and considered him a friend. He referred to him as "Brooklyn Jack, a hustling, romantic poet of the streets." But Hank also described Jack as a "screamer" and someone who protested his fate too much.

Hank talked about Jack visiting him in Los Angeles and their drinking bouts. Hank seemed put off that Jack would often bring with him a "stack" of poems. He said he didn't want to listen to the poetry of others (good or bad), but said Jack was one of the few poets who had inspired him to write a poem about them.

Hank said he occasionally wrote a poem "slamming" a poet, but seldom wrote a poem praising one, as he had done with Jack. Hank felt a lot of Jack's letters were like poems.

"How can I not like a man who enjoys going to the race track as much as Jack does?" Hank asked.

Linda King would occasionally break in with a laugh, throwing her arms around Hank and saying, "He's OK. He's all right, but he's no Buk."

As the evening wore on, Hank and Linda said they were retiring for the evening. As I recall, Hank simply stood up and said, "It's time to call it a night." I felt like I was being dismissed from the King's court.

RB wanted to stay the night, but Hank said no, at the same time whispering to me I was free to return and sleep at Linda's home, after I got rid of RB. I thanked Hank, but suffering from insomnia and finding it hard to sleep on couches, I politely declined the offer.

As I stood there at the open door, preparing to head out into the night, I paused to look Hank in the eye. I informed him Harold Norse had warned me that someday he (Hank) would turn against me, even as he had done with Norse and others.

I repeated Norse's often spoken remark that Hank couldn't stand to be loved, which drew a familiar impish smile that Hank was famous for.

"And I will," he said.

"No, you won't, "I said. My remark seemed to catch him off guard. He wanted to know why I felt he would not turn on me.

"Because," I said, "what you said about the others was true, you don't know anything bad about me."

"You're right," Hank said, embracing me in a bear hug.

As I departed Linda's home, I watched her wave from behind the window, as I left with RB for the hotel room I had rented for the night. There followed nearly two decades of personal correspondence between Hank and myself, along with infrequent telephone conversations, which turned to silence after Hank made the big time.

Jack Micheline and A.D. Winans. San Francisco. 1990.

A.D. Winans Biography.

A. D. Winans is a native San Francisco award winning poet and writer.

He is the author of over sixty books of poetry and prose, including *North Beach Poems, North Beach Revisited, Billie Holiday Me And The Blues, Drowning Like Li Po in a River of Red Wine, In The Dead Hours of Dawn, Love – Zero, San Francisco Poems, In The Pink, and On My Way To Becoming A Man.*

In 2006 He won a PEN Josephine Miles Award for Excellence in Literature. In 2009 PEN Oakland awarded him a lifetime achievement award. His name is on a plaque in North Beach with other poets and artists who have contributed to the North Beach literary scene, including Francis Ford Coppola, Allen Ginsberg, Lawrence Ferlinghetti, Jack Micheline, and other major Beat poets and writers.

From 1972 to 1989 Winans edited and published Second Coming Press, which produced a large number of books and anthologies, among them the highly acclaimed California *Bicentennial Poet's Anthology, which included poets like David Meltzer, Jack Micheline, Lawrence Ferlinghetti, Ishmael Reed, Josephine Miles, Bob Kaufman, and William Everson.*

He worked as an editor and writer for the San Francisco Art Commission, Neighborhood Arts Program, from 1975 to 1980, during which time he produced the Second Coming 1980 Poets and Music Festival, honoring the late Josephine Miles and John Lee Hooker.

He was an active participant in the Folsom Prison Writer's Workshop and other prison writing programs.

His work has appeared in over 1500 literary magazines and anthologies, including City Lights Journal, Exquisite Corpse, Poetry Australia, Confrontation, The New York Quarterly, The Patterson Literary Review, The San Francisco Chronicle, and The Outlaw Bible of American Poetry.

In April 2002 a poem of his was set to music By William Bolcom, a Pulitzer Prize winning composer, and performed at New York's Alice Tully Hall.

In 2012 The Louisiana University at Lafayette recorded a CD of Song Cycles by American Composers, and included in the CD is the song cycle of nationally acclaimed William Bolcom. *Old* Addresses, with song poems by Winans, Oscar Wilde, Ezra Pound, Langston Hughes, C.P. Cavafy, Kenneth Koch and others.

Writers like Colin Wilson, Studs Terkel, James Purdy, Peter Coyote, Herbert Gold, and the late Jack Micheline and Charles Bukowski have praised his work.

He has worked at a variety of jobs, most recently with the U.S. Dept. of Education as an Equal Opportunity Specialist, investigating claims of discrimination against minorities, women and the disabled.

Winans is a member of PEN, and has served on the Board of Directors of various art organizations, including the now defunct Committee of Small Magazine Editors and Publishers (COSMEP).

His essay on the late Bob Kaufman was published in the American Poetry Review and was republished in 2007 by The Writer's Research Group.   In September 2009 the article was again re-published along with a poem of his for Bob Kaufman, as part of a booklet produced by the Los Angeles Afro American Museum.

OTHER BOOKS BY A.D. WINANS

Carmel Clowns (1970)
Crazy John Poems (1972)
Straws Of Sanity (1975)
Tales of Crazy John (1975)
North Beach Poems (1977)
ORG-1 (Scarecrow 1977)
All the Graffiti On All The Bathroom Walls
Can't Hide These Scars (1977)
The Further Adventures of Crazy John (1979)
The Reagan Psalms (1984)
In Memoriam (1990)
A Knife In the Heart And Jazz In My Soul (1996)
This Land Is Not My Land (1996)
The Charles Bukowski Second Coming Years (1996)
Love Comes In Many Different Flavors (1996)
It Serves You Right To Suffer (1996)
A Call To Poets (1997)
Venus In Pisces (1997)
Remembering Jack Micheline (1998)
America (1998)
Looking For An Answer (1998)
San Francisco Streets (1998)
From Pussy To Politics (1999)
Folk Heroes & Other Strange Happenings (1999)
Remembering Bukowski (1999)
Scar Tissue (1999)
People You think You Know (1999)
Poems for the Poet The Working Man
And The Downtrodden (1999)
North Beach Revisited (2000)
13 Jazz Poems (2000)
City Blues (2001)
I Kiss The Feet Of Angels (2001)
The Holy Grail: Charles Bukowski And The
 Second Coming Revolution. (2002)
Whispers From Hell (2002)
Will the Real Lawrence Ferlinghetti
Please Stand Up (2002)
Trying To Find A Common Bond (2002)
A Bastard Child With No Place To Go (2002)
The System (2003)
A.D. Winans' Greatest Hits: 1995-2003 (2003)

Sleeping With Demons (2003)
Whitman's Lost Children (2004)
Dreams That Won't Leave Me Alone (2004)
In Memoriam: New and Selected Poems (2004)
The Wrong Side Of Town (2005)
This Land Is Not My Land (2005)
The Other Side Of Broadway:
Selected Poems: 1965-2005 (2007)
The World's Last Rodeo (2006)
South of Market Street (2006)
Marking Time (2008)
No Room For Buddha (2009)
Days In Heaven Nights In Hell (2009)
Billie Holiday Me And The Blues (2009)
Pigeon Feathers (2009)
Dancing With Words (2010)
Love Minus Zero (2010)
Black Lily (2010)
Drowning Like Li Po in a River of Red Wine:
Selected Poems: 1970-2010 (2010)
San Francisco Poems (2011)
Wind On His Wings (2012)
In the Dead Hours of Dawn (2012)
In The Pink (2014)
On My Way To Becoming A Man (2014)
This Land Is Not My Land
Second Edition (2014)

Other Punk Hostage Press Titles

Fractured (2012) by Danny Baker

Better Than A gun In A Knife Fight (2012) by A. Razor

The Daughters of Bastards (2012) by Iris Berry

Drawn Blood: Collected Works from D.B.P.Ltd., 1985-1995 (2012) by A. Razor

impress (2012) by C.V. Auchterlonie

Tomorrow, Yvonne- Poetry & Prose for Suicidal Egoists (2012) by Yvonne De la Vega

Beaten Up Beaten Down (2012) by A. Razor

miracles of the BloG: A series (2012) by Carolyn Srygley-Moore

8th & Agony (2012) by Rich Ferguson

Untamed (2013) by Jack Grisham

Moth Wing Tea (2013) by Dennis Cruz

Half-Century Status (2013) by A.Razor

Showgirl Confidential (2013) by Pleasant Gehma

Blood Music (2013) by Frank Reardon

I Will Always Be Your Whore (2013) by Alexandra Naughton

A History of Broken Love Things (2014) by SB Stokes

Yeah Well (2104) by Joel Landmine

Code Blue: A Love Story (2014) by Jack Grisham

Dreams Gone Mad with Hope (2014) by S.A. Griffin

Forthcoming from Punk Hostage Press

When I Was A Dynamiter (2014) by Lee Quarnstrom

Where The Road Leads You (2014) by Diana Rose

Disgraceland (2014) by Iris Berry & Pleasant Gehamn

Long Winded Tales of a Low Plains Drifter (2014)
by A.Razor

Boulevard of Spoken Dreams (2014) by Iris Berry

Dangerous Intersections (2014) by Annette Cruz

Driving All of the Horses at Once (2014) by Richard Modiano

The Red Hook Giraffe (2014)
by James Anthony Tropeano III

Shooting For The Stars In Kevlar by Iris Berry

Puro Purismo (2014) by A. Razor

Made in the USA
San Bernardino, CA
08 November 2014